Word for Windows™ Hot Tips

George R. Beinhorn

que

Word for Windows Hot Tips

Library of Congress Catalog No.: 92-84093

ISBN: 1-56529-163-8

96 95 94 93   4 3 2 1

Interpretation of the printing code: the rightmost double-digit number is the year of the book's printing; the rightmost single-digit number, the number of the book's printing. For example, a printing code of 93-1 shows that the first printing of the book occurred in 1993.

Word for Windows Hot Tips is based on Microsoft® Word for Windows™ Version 2.0.

Trademark Acknowledgments

Que Corporation has made every effort to supply trademark information about company names, products, and services mentioned in this book. Trademarks indicated below were derived from various sources. Que Corporation cannot attest to the accuracy of this information.

Microsoft Excel, MS-DOS, Microsoft Windows, Microsoft Word, and Microsoft Word for Windows are registered trademarks of Microsoft Corporation.

dBASE is a registered trademark of Borland International, Inc.

Credits

Publisher
Lloyd J. Short

Associate Publisher
Rick Ranucci

Operations Manager
Sheila Cunningham

Publishing Plan Manager
Thomas H. Bennett

Title Manager
Shelley O'Hara

Product Director
Robin Drake

Acquisitions Editor
Sarah Browning

Production Editor
Anne Owen

Copy Editors
William A. Barton
Elsa M. Bell
Fran Blauw

Technical Editor
Lynda Fox

Production Team
Jeff Baker
Julie Brown
Jodie Cantwell
Paula Carroll
Laurie Casey
Michelle Cleary
Brook Farling
Heather Kaufman
Bob LaRoche
Linda Seifert
Sandra Shay

Indexer
Tina Trettin

Composed in *Utopia* and *MCPdigital* by Que Corporation.

About The Author

George R. Beinhorn is a writer, editor, and commercial photographer. He is the author of Que's *Using Professional Write Plus for Windows, Look Your Best with WordPerferct for Windows,* and is the revision author of *Using Q & A,* 4th Edition. He writes the "Pro Tips" word processing column for *PC Computing* magazine.

Beinhorn serves as a document design consultant for business clients and may be reached through Que Corporation.

Table of Contents

Introduction

Whether you're a beginning or experienced Word for Windows user, the shortcuts and powerful techniques presented in *Word for Windows Hot Tips* will help improve your proficiency. In this book, you find information about the subtle program features you were too busy to read about in the documentation. You also find undocumented secrets, tips, and proven advice.

Unlike some computer books, it's not necessary to read the chapters or tips in this book in any particular order. Each chapter includes tips for a particular feature or function of Word for Windows.

Watch, in particular, for tips identified by a "Hot" icon. These tips are the author's favorites and are bound to pique your interest. You can find a list of these tips on the inside front and back covers of this book.

If you want a comprehensive overview of Word for Windows, pick up a copy of Que's *Using Word for Windows 2,* Special Edition.

Book Conventions

Certain conventions are used in *Word for Windows Hot Tips* to help you understand the techniques and features described in the text. This section provides examples of these conventions.

Words printed in uppercase include DOS commands (CHKDSK) and file names (STATUS.DOC). The following table shows special formatting used in this book.

Format	Meaning
italics	Emphasized text and variables
boldface	Hot keys for menu options and words user types
`special typeface`	Direct quotations of words that appear on-screen or in a figure; menu command prompts

In most cases, keys are represented as they appear on the keyboard. The Print Screen key is abbreviated PrtSc, Page Up is PgUp, Insert is Ins, and so on; on your keyboard, these key names may be spelled out or abbreviated differently.

Throughout the text, the term *Enter* is used instead of *Return* for the Enter key.

Ctrl+F1 indicates that you press the Ctrl key and hold it down while you press the F1 key. Other key combinations (such as Alt+Esc) are performed in the same manner. If key combinations aren't indicated with a plus sign (+), don't hold down any of the keys; press each key once in the order listed (for example, End Home).

Where applicable, buttons in the margin indicate that the text includes instructions for using that button.

1 CHAPTER

Word for Windows Basics

Word provides all the benefits of the Microsoft Word graphical environment, including the capability to switch to other applications by using a few keystrokes and to have Word automatically update data imported into a document from another application when the source data changes. The Word editing screen enables you to load up to nine documents at once and to work in Normal, Page Layout, or Draft screen modes. (With Word 2.0 and later versions, you can switch to a character-based screen for fast editing.) This chapter provides tips for understanding and optimizing the Word window to better meet your document-creation needs.

Use Shift+F1 when F1 doesn't work

Word's F1 (Help) key is inactive in certain menus and dialog boxes. When this is the case, try pressing Shift+F1, which turns the mouse cursor into a question mark. Click the question mark on the dialog box or on any other area of the screen. Word provides Help on that feature if it's available. Press Esc to change the question mark back to the standard mouse cursor. (Exception: Pressing Shift + F1 when WordPerfect Help is enabled takes you to the WordPerfect Help screen. To use the question mark cursor, you must disable WordPerfect Help.)

Jump between Help and the on-screen document

To make editing changes or to experiment with features while you're using Word's Help system, press Alt+Esc or click the Minimize button in the Help window to return to the on-screen document temporarily. To return to the previous Help screen, press Alt+Esc again.

Print Help topics for reference

Word can print a neatly formatted copy of any Help topic. To print a topic, display the topic and choose File Print Topic.

Get Help for grayed menu items

Sometimes it's convenient to display Help for a menu item that is grayed (not currently available). In such cases, selecting the menu item and pressing F1 (Help) doesn't work. Instead, select the grayed command by using the keyboard and press F1. Or point to the command, hold down the left mouse button, and press F1.

Use a bookmark to mark Help screens

If you must refer repeatedly to the same Help screen, you can mark the screen with a bookmark and jump to it immediately. Open the Help screen and choose Bookmark Define, give the bookmark a name, and choose OK. To return to the menu, choose Help Help Index Bookmark and select the Help screen by name. To shorten the process even further, record a macro that displays the Help Bookmark menu.

Customize Help

If you call Microsoft's WinWord help line and learn information that isn't included in the User's Guide, you can place the information in an on-line Help screen for easy reference. Display the Help screen to which you want to add the information, choose Edit Annotate, type the note, and choose Save. Word places a paper clip symbol to the left of the Help screen's title to remind you that you have created an annotation. To display the note, choose Edit Annotate.

Find Help on topics not included in the User's Guide

Many topics not covered in the Word User's Guide are described in Help screens. For example, detailed instructions for field statements and WordBasic programming commands are available through the Help system. To get Help for a field statement, follow these steps:

1. Choose Insert Field and highlight the field's name in the Insert Field Type list box, and then press F1.

   or

   Choose Help Help Index Search, type **fields**, press Tab, move the cursor to fields: an overview, and press Enter twice.

2. In the Fields Help screen, choose Field Types and Instructions to display a list of fields.

3. Press Tab to highlight a field name and press Enter to display detailed instructions for using the field. You also can click the field name by using the mouse.

4. Choose File Print Topic to print the instructions.

With most printers, the Help text is beautifully formatted and printed. If this is not the case with your printer, copy the Help text to the Word window and print the text as document text.

To get Help with WordBasic programming language functions and statements, follow these steps:

1. Choose Help Help Index.
2. Choose WordBasic Programming Language.
3. In the WordBasic Programming Language Help screen, click the name of a function or command. Word displays a Help screen for the chosen item.
4. Choose File Print Topic to print the instructions.

You also can display help for WordBasic topics cross-referenced by category. Follow these steps:

1. Choose Help Help Index.
2. Choose WordBasic Programming Language.
3. In the WordBasic Programming Language Help screen, click the WordBasic Cross Reference hot key.

Use Alt+F4 to close Help quickly

To close Help dialog boxes and screens quickly, press Alt+F4.

Use the mouse to display the description of a tool

To find out what a Toolbar button does, point to the button and hold down the left mouse button. A description of the tool appears in the bottom left corner of the screen (status bar). To avoid activating the button, move the cursor off the Toolbar before releasing the mouse button.

Work with two copies of the same document

Word enables you to open as many as nine documents at once in separate editing windows. You even can open multiple copies of the same document. Any changes you make in one copy of the document are simultaneously made in the other copies.

A useful application for opening two views of the same document is to check the results of editing changes in *field codes.* Use the following steps to apply this method:

1. To open a copy of the document, choose File Open.
2. To open a second copy of the document, choose File Open again.
3. Drag the split mark at the top of the vertical scroll bar to split the screen so you can view both documents at the same time.
4. In the currently active window, choose View Field Codes to turn on the display of field codes.
5. Locate the field code you want to edit.
6. Press Ctrl+F6 to switch to another document window. Scroll to the field code in this window, but leave the display of field codes turned off. (Only field results are displayed.)
7. Press Ctrl+Shift+F6 as many times as necessary to switch back to the first window. Edit the field code and press F9 to update the field.

   Notice that the new field code results appear in the second window. Displaying field codes and results prevents you from having to toggle field codes on and off to check results.

Open several documents at once

When you need to work with several documents simultaneously, it's quickest to open all the files at the same time. You can't perform this action from the Open dialog box (**File Open**). To open several files at once, follow these steps:

1. Choose **File Find File**.
2. Choose **Search** to locate the desired group of files and choose **Start Search**.

   or

   Hold down Ctrl while you click the file names of up to nine files in the File Name list.

   By using the mouse, highlight the first file name and press Shift + F8. Then move to the next document you want and press the space bar to select the document. Press the space bar for each document you want to open. To deselect a file name, highlight it and press the space bar again.
3. Choose **Open** to open all the files, each in its own window.

Use screen colors even if your printer can't print in color

To make key text stand out on-screen, you can highlight the text with colors. The on-screen colors have no effect on the document when you print it on a black-and-white printer. To highlight text, follow these steps:

1. Select the text you want to appear in color.
2. Choose **Format Character**.
3. Choose a color from the **Color** list and choose **OK**.

You can use this technique to make phone numbers and other key information stand out from surrounding text.

Assign colors/enhancements to toolbar buttons/shortcut keys

You can assign colors and other character enhancements to a toolbar button or shortcut key. Follow these steps to choose a shortcut key:

1. Choose Tools Options and press K to display the Keyboard options.
2. Choose Show Commands.
3. In the Commands list, choose CharColor.
4. Select a shortcut key in the Shortcut Key box.
5. Choose Add and then choose Close.

When you press the shortcut key, Word displays `Which color?` in the status bar. Type a color name and press Enter. You can type color names listed when you choose Format Character Color. Word applies the color to any selected text or to the next text you type.

Write notes to yourself in the document text

Word enables you to display nonprinting notes in the document screen. Follow these steps to type nonprinting notes:

1. Press Ctrl+H.
2. Type the text.

Hidden text appears with a dotted underline.

To permanently turn on the display of hidden text, choose Tools Options View and select the Hidden Text check box or the All check box in the Nonprinting Characters box.

You can tell Word to include hidden text in the printed document. Choose File Print Options and select the Hidden Text check box.

You can make printing hidden text the default. Choose Tools Options Print and select the Hidden Text check box. With the Hidden Text check box selected in the Print Options dialog box, Word displays hidden text in the Print Preview screen if it appears in the document screen.

Toggling hidden text on and off quickly

A quicker way to toggle hidden text on and off is by clicking the paragraph button at the right end of the ribbon. It's a good idea to perform this action before printing the document because hidden text displaces page breaks, margins, and other page elements when displayed. To make your notes stand out on-screen, format them in color as described earlier.

To print a document without printing hidden text, choose File Print Options, deselect the Hidden Text check box, and choose OK.

Use draft mode for fast screen updates

Use Draft mode for fast text entry and switch to Page Layout mode when it's time to fine-tune your page layouts. Word updates the screen faster when you work in Draft mode. This option is especially helpful for documents that contain many fonts in various type sizes and frames, graphic images, and field codes. To switch to Draft mode, choose View Draft.

For even faster screen updating, turn on the display of field codes to display embedded drawings and other graphic objects as fields. Choose View Field Codes. With field codes turned on, for example, a Microsoft Draw object is displayed as a field:

```
{EMBED MSDraw \* mergeformat}
```

Create a Zoom button

Zooming the on-screen document takes four mouse clicks or four keystrokes: choose View Zoom, select a screen size, and choose OK. The following, seldom-mentioned customization option enables you to exchange the Zoom 100% toolbar button for a nifty Zoom tool that you can drag by using the mouse to scale the display from 25% to 200%.

Follow these steps to create a Zoom Toolbar button:

1. Choose **F**ile **N**ew, choose the NORMAL template, and choose OK.
2. Choose T**o**ols **O**ptions and press **t** to display the Toolbar options.
3. In the **T**ool to Change box, choose ViewZoom100.
4. In the Show box, choose C**o**mmands.
5. In the Commands list, choose ViewZoom.
6. Choose Ch**a**nge and then choose Close.

   When you click the Zoom tool, Word displays a downward-pointing arrow. Drag the mouse cursor along the arrow to select a zoom percentage and release the mouse button.

7. When you exit Word, choose **Y**es at the prompt to save your changes.

Display a ruler in header and footer panes

Word doesn't display a ruler in the *header editing pane* or *footer editing pane*, but you can trick it into doing so. Follow these steps:

1. Choose View Header/Footer.
2. Choose Header or Footer and any options.
3. Choose OK.

   Word opens the header or footer pane.
4. Choose View Ruler.

   Word turns off the ruler in the editing window.
5. Choose View Ruler again.

   Word displays a ruler in the Header or Footer pane. When you close the pane, the ruler returns to the editing window.

Switch to Page Layout view to accurately position frames

You should be aware that Normal and Draft views don't accurately show the position of frames on the page. In Normal and Draft views, frames appear as small black boxes.

To accurately position frames, switch to Page Layout view by choosing View Page Layout.

If double-clicking a frame doesn't display its sizing handles, you're probably working in Normal or Draft View.

Adjust the page width to fit text within the display margins

Word may sometimes display text lines that extend beyond the right edge of the screen. To correct this problem, try the following solutions:

1. Choose Tools Options and choose View in the Category box. Deselect the Line Breaks and Fonts as Printed check box and choose OK.

   If the Line Breaks and Fonts as Printed item is grayed, return to the editing screen and choose View Normal to turn on normal view, then repeat step 1.

2. Choose View Zoom Page Width.

   or

   Click the Page Width button at the far right end of the toolbar.

Avoid using symbol fonts instead of text fonts

If Word displays a symbol font instead of a text font such as Times Roman, the problem may be because you're using a printer driver for an HP LaserJet printer.

To fix the problem, try these solutions:

1. Install a font cartridge or a soft font that includes the text font you want to use.

   or

   Choose Tools Options View.

2. Deselect the Line Breaks and Fonts as Printed check box and choose OK.

If the Line Breaks and Fonts as Printed item is grayed, return to the editing screen and choose View Normal to turn on normal view, then repeat step 1.

Display the document as it will print

For a screen display that most accurately reflects how your documents will print, follow these steps:

1. Choose Tools Options and press V to display View options.
2. Make sure that the Line Breaks and Fonts as Printed check box is selected.

Use the PrtScr key with a Word menu displayed

If you try to print a Word screen by pressing Alt+PrtSc with a menu displayed, the Alt key will cause the drop-down menu to disappear. To print the current Word screen including the menu, follow these steps:

1. Hold down Alt and press the key for the menu that you want to display, and then release the menu key. Without releasing Alt, press the PrtSc key.

   The screen is now on the Clipboard.

2. Choose Edit Paste (Ctrl+V) to insert the image from the Clipboard into Word's editing window.
3. Choose File Print and choose OK to print the screen.

You can save the screen image in a file for printing later or for inclusion in other files. To save the file in a format that Word can read, don't use the Clipboard editor's Save As function because Word cannot open Clipboard files. Instead, paste the image as described in steps 1–3, then save the file as a Word document (choose File Save As, type a file name, and choose OK).

2

CHAPTER

Editing Word Documents

Word has an amazingly rich variety of editing tools. You can perform many editing functions by using the mouse, menus, shortcut keys, and toolbar buttons or by double-clicking an empty space in the toolbar, ribbon, ruler, or status bar. The tips in this chapter will help you become aware of ways to use these tools more efficiently.

For a quick review of Word's many editing commands, follow these steps:

1. Choose Help Help Index.
2. To find help for an underlined feature, click its text or highlight it by pressing Tab, and then press Enter.

   Word displays a list of keyboard and mouse functions. To review a specific function group (for example, character formatting key combinations), click the hot text.
3. For a neatly formatted printout of a Help screen, choose File Print Topic.

Find your place after moving the cursor

When you open a document, press Shift+F5 (Go Back) to return to where you were working when you last saved the file. Word stores the last three working locations. To move through these locations, press Shift+F5 again. This capability is tremendously useful for moving or copying text and returning quickly to the place where you selected the text.

Replace text safely

Before using Replace, save your document. Word can reverse a replace operation if you choose **E**dit **U**ndo (Ctrl+Z) immediately after the replace operation, but not after you perform any editing operations. In order to use Undo after using Replace, you cannot confirm each replacement; you must choose Replace **A**ll. If you confirm each replacement (by choosing **F**ind Next), choosing **U**ndo restores only the last replacement.

Replace long text

You can specify no more than 255 characters of text in the Replace With box. To insert longer text by using Replace, copy the text to the Clipboard. In the Edit menu Replace With box, type **^c** (caret c). (Don't press Ctrl+C.) This technique may be useful for replacing boilerplate sections of a contract or for replacing a graphic image with another image from the Clipboard.

Replace character enhancements

You can find and replace character enhancements such as boldface, italic, and underlining. In the Find What or Replace With box, type the shortcut key for the enhancement. To change boldfaced text to italic, for example, follow these steps:

1. Choose Edit Replace.
2. In the Find What box, press Ctrl+B.

   Word doesn't show anything in the Find What box, but displays `Bold` at the `Format:` prompt.
3. In the Replace With box, press Ctrl+I.

   Word displays Italic at the `Format:` prompt.
4. Choose Find Next or Replace All to begin changing boldface text to italic.
5. To remove all enhancements, press the shortcut key in the Find What box, but leave the Replace With box blank.

To replace all text that is not italic (or bold, underlined, and so on), press the shortcut key twice in the Find What box. For example, press Ctrl+I twice and Word displays `Not Italic` at the `Format:` prompt. This trick is useful when you have a document that is formatted primarily with italic or bold and you want to change any unitalicized text or unboldfaced text.

For a list of other special search/replace characters, see page 265 in the User's Guide. Note that the characters in the list are entered by typing **^n** (caret n), for example, not by pressing Ctrl and a letter, as for undocumented codes.

Make editing easier with heading styles

If you see that you will need to change the order of text in a long document, you can save time by formatting headings with heading styles from the NORMAL template. (To apply NORMAL, choose the Template button, then choose

Normal in the Use Template list in the New dialog box, displayed when you choose **File New**.) To reorganize the document, choose **View Outline** and change the order of text by moving headings in Outline view.

Use special search characters

With Find or Replace, you can type the codes from the following table in the Find What and Replace With boxes to search for the items indicated. To insert the caret character (^), press Shift+6 on the alphanumeric keyboard.

Code	Finds
^1	Picture
^2	Footnote
^3	Footnote separator
^5	Annotation mark
^7	End-of-table-cell marker
^9	Tab
^10	Linefeed
^11	Newline (Shift+Enter)
^12	Page or section break
^13	Carriage return (paragraph mark)
^14	Column break
^19	Field start
^21	Field end
?	Any single character (not valid in Replace text)
^?	Question mark
^w	White space: space, nonbreaking space, tab
^t	Tab
^p	Paragraph mark

Code	Finds
^n	Newline (Shift+Enter)
^d	Section mark
^s	Nonbreaking space
^-	Optional (soft) hyphen
^~	Nonbreaking hyphen
^^	Caret
^m	Duplicates the search text (Replace only)
^c	Replace with Clipboard contents (Replace only)
^nnn	ASCII character number nnn
^0nnn	Windows ANSI character number nnn

Use drag-and-drop

If you're new to Word 2.0, you may not be familiar with the wonderful new drag-and-drop feature. Following are examples of how it works:

To move a graphic image, follow these steps:

1. Position the cursor on the graphic so that a four-pronged arrow appears.
2. Drag-and-drop the graphic to a new position on the page. Click the graphic and hold down the mouse button while you move the mouse cursor to the new location, then release the mouse button to "drop" the object in its new location.

To move text, follow these steps:

1. Select the text you want to use; for example, double-click a paragraph to select it.

2. Drag-and-drop the text to a new position.

You can drag-and-drop text or graphics anywhere in a document.

Automate repetitive typing tasks

To automate repetitive typing tasks, like repeating Los Angeles, CA 90065, or to insert longer boilerplate paragraphs, you can use Word's glossary feature. You can use glossary entries to retrieve single words or large chunks of text, complete with formatting. You also can make glossary entries available for use with all documents or with specific document templates.

Because the glossary feature is rich and complex, it's not within the scope of this book to describe it in detail. To create a simple glossary entry, follow these steps:

1. Select the text you want to insert repeatedly.

   If you want to include formatting, be sure to select paragraph marks.

2. Choose **Edit Glossary**, type a glossary name, and choose **Define**.

3. To insert a glossary item, choose **Edit Glossary**, choose the item from the Glossary Name list, and choose **Insert**.

   To insert the glossary item and apply the formatting of surrounding text, choose **Insert As Plain Text**.

   or

   In the text of your document, type the name of the glossary item and press F3. Word replaces the glossary name with the glossary item.

Search for page breaks and section breaks

You can search for Word's page breaks and section breaks, but you must first turn on the display of nonprinting characters:

1. Choose Tools Options, press V to choose the View category, select All in the Nonprinting Characters box, and choose OK.
2. Choose Edit Find. In the Find What box, type one of the characters from the following table to locate each type of break.

To Find	Type
Column Break	^0014
Ctrl+Shift+Enter	^0014
Hard Page Break	^0012 or ^d
Next Page Break	^0012 or ^d
Continuous Break	^0012 or ^d
Odd Page Break	^0012 or ^d
Even Page Break	^0012 or ^d

Append documents easily

To include the contents of another document in the document you're creating, use the INCLUDE command. Follow these steps:

1. Position the cursor where you want to insert another document.
2. Press Ctrl+F9 to insert empty field brackets.

3. In the field brackets, type **INCLUDE** and the name of the document you want to insert:

   {INCLUDE document}

When you print the document, Word inserts the indicated document at the location of the INCLUDE field.

Copy text from a Word document to a DOS application

If you run DOS programs under Windows, you occasionally may want to copy text from Word to a DOS application. To perform this task, follow these steps:

1. In the DOS application, position the cursor at the point where you want to paste text from Word.
2. Press Alt+Tab to return to Word. Select the text and choose Edit Copy (Ctrl+C).
3. Click the icon for the DOS application, then choose Edit Paste. Windows pastes the text on the Clipboard at the location of the cursor in the DOS application.

Move blocks of text quickly

To move text or graphics quickly, select the text or the graphic, position the cursor where you want to insert the text or graphic, and hold down Ctrl while you click the right mouse button.

Gather blocks of text at a single location

What's the quickest way to move blocks of text from various locations in a long document without scrolling to and from the new location? Selecting text and then choosing Edit Cut or Edit Copy replaces any text currently on the Clipboard, so you can't gather text with the Clipboard. (If you accidentally replace the Clipboard contents, choose Edit Undo to restore the previous Clipboard contents.)

The *Spike feature* can only cut text, not move it; nor can you append selected text to a glossary item or a file. (The Spike is a special glossary entry that is similar to the Clipboard. Unlike the Clipboard, which holds only one entry at a time, you can cut text and gather it on the Spike without replacing the existing contents, then insert the contents of the Spike at a new location.)

One way to gather text is by opening a second window and using the drag-and-drop feature (new to Word for Windows 2.0) to gather blocks in the second document.

To open a second document window and gather text there, follow these steps:

1. Choose Window New Window.
2. Choose Window Arrange All.
3. Open a document in the first window and select the first block of text.
4. Move the mouse cursor into the second window. Without clicking a mouse button to move the insertion point to the second window, press Ctrl+Shift and click the right mouse button.

   Word copies the selected text to the second window. (To move text, hold down Ctrl, point to the new location with the mouse cursor, and click the right mouse button.)
5. Press Enter to insert a blank line after the text and repeat the process.
6. When you have collected all the blocks, press Ctrl+5 (from the keypad) to select the contents of the second window.

7. Point with the mouse cursor to the insertion point in the first window, hold down Ctrl+Shift, and click the right mouse button.

Move and copy text

An easy way to simplify moving and copying selected text is by bypassing the Clipboard by using the Move and Copy keys. These keys aren't documented in on-line help, and they are only briefly described in the User's Guide.

The Move and Copy keys enable you to move or copy text and jump back immediately to your previous location. Follow these steps:

1. Move the insertion point where you want the moved or copied text to be inserted.
2. Press F2 to move text or Shift+F2 to copy text.

   Word displays `Move from where?` or `Copy from where?` in the status bar.
3. Select the text you want to move or copy. The selected text is underlined.
4. Press Enter to move or copy the text.

Word inserts the text and moves the insertion point to the original location. You can use any Word selection process with this method, such as clicking in the selection bar, double-clicking a word, and so on.

Alternatively, you can select text and press F2 (Move) or Shift+F2 (Copy), click at the new insertion point, and press Enter. To gather text at a single location, use this procedure repeatedly. Between copy/move repetitions, return to the previous location by pressing the Go Back key (Shift+F5).

Use styles to collect text

To shorten the process of collecting text blocks of no more than 255 characters each at a single location in a document, follow these steps:

1. Format the text blocks with standard header style number 9, which you probably would seldom use.
2. Move the insertion point where you want to collect the text.
3. Insert a table of contents that contains only heading level 9. Choose Insert Table of Contents, choose Use Heading Paragraphs, specify 9 in the From: and To: boxes, and choose OK.

Word inserts the marked text blocks at the insertion point. Remember that this method is limited to copying blocks of no more than 255 characters. Also remember that to include a table of contents and other automatically generated lists in the same document, you must mark list entries with fields, as described in the User's Guide.

Use annotations to gather text

Another way to collect text at the end of a document is to designate each section of text you want to gather as an annotation. Follow these steps:

1. Choose Insert Annotation.

   Word opens the annotation pane where you can create an annotation.

2. Copy the text to the annotation pane.
3. Repeat steps 1 and 2 for each block of text you want to gather.
4. Move the cursor to where you want to insert the gathered text.
5. Choose Insert Annotation.

6. In the annotation pane, select each annotation field code and press Del.
7. Copy the gathered text into the document.
8. To print annotations, choose File Print Options and choose the Annotations check box.

Word prints annotations on a separate page at the end of the document.

Select columnar blocks of text and numbers

When working with columns of text separated with tabs (columns of numbers, for example; not newspaper-style columns or tables), remember that you can select columns of text with the right mouse button. Word extends the selection in columnar fashion—not from margin to margin, as when you select text with the left mouse button.

You can perform the same cut, copy, and paste operations on columnar blocks as you would for blocks of text selected with the left mouse button. When cutting, copying, or moving columnar text, remember to include the tabs that follow a column so you retain correct spacing between columns when you paste the block.

Select text by using keyboard shortcuts

The following shortcut keys simplify selecting text with the keyboard and mouse:

Keyboard:

Hold down Shift and use cursor movement keys to select text.

or

Press F8 repeatedly to select a word, sentence, paragraph, section, or the entire document. To back up through the selection steps, press Shift+F8, or press Esc to turn off extended selection mode.

Mouse:

Selected text	Action
A word	Double-click the word
A paragraph	Double-click the selection bar*
The entire document	Hold down Ctrl and click the selection bar*

** The selection bar is at the left edge of the text area. When the mouse cursor is in the selection bar, the cursor is an arrow.*

Use the F8 key to select, delete, and extend sections

To delete a sentence quickly, press F8 three times, then press Del.

To extend a selection, you can press F8 and use Search Go To, or any cursor movement key.

To select several sentences, press F8 once, then press period several times.

To select several paragraphs, press F8, then press Enter several times. (To move the current paragraph up or down in a document, first select the paragraph with F8 as described in the preceding sentence, then press Shift+Alt+up arrow or Shift+Alt+down arrow.)

Use the split bar to split and remove the screen

To split the screen quickly, double-click the split bar. To remove the split screen, double-click the split bar in the vertical scroll bar. (The split bar is the small black rectangle above the Vertical Scroll bar up arrow, not the line separating the two windows.)

Save time with Word's quick-click mouse commands

You can save time by using the following Word mouse commands:

Double-click here	To perform this action
Status bar	Display the Go To dialog box
Blank areas of the ribbon	Display the Format Character dialog box
Ruler	Display the Format Paragraph dialog box
Selection bar	Select a line with one click; select a paragraph with two clicks

Exit Print Preview quickly

To exit Print Preview quickly, double-click anywhere outside the icon bar and scroll bar.

View the Clipboard

To view the contents of the Windows Clipboard, press Alt, space bar, choose Run, and OK. Windows displays the Clipboard Viewer.

View Page Preview quickly

For a quick look at the current page that closely approximates the final, printed version, in Page Layout View click the Zoom Whole Page button (it's at the right end of the toolbar in Word as installed). This step is quicker than using Print Preview or View Zoom, and you can perform normal editing functions such as cutting and pasting (which aren't possible in Print Preview). To switch back to normal page view, click the 100% Normal view Toolbar button (it's the second button from the right end of the Toolbar in Word as installed).

View and return quickly

To view a distant area of a document and return immediately to the place where you were working, use the vertical scroll bar to move to the new area, then press the space bar and press Backspace to remove the space. Word redisplays the area in which you were working.

Scroll into the margins

To scroll horizontally into the left and right margins, hold down Shift while you click the left or right scroll arrow.

Use mouse clicks as shortcuts

To quickly display the Format Character dialog box, double-click in a space between buttons on the ribbon or press Ctrl+F or Ctrl+P twice. To display the Options dialog box from the Tools menu, double-click in a space between toolbar buttons.

Create fill-in forms easily

A quick way to create fill-in forms for return coupons and other response forms is to create a table with a row for each line in the form and only one column. Follow these steps:

1. Choose Table Insert Table and specify one column and the desired number of rows. (Don't use the table tool in the toolbar because you need to specify a fixed column width.)

2. Set Column Width to the desired width of the fill-in form and choose OK.

3. Type the data entry prompts (Name, Address, and so on), adjust their positions with the space bar, and check your results with Print Preview.

4. Select a column to format, then format the cells by choosing Format Border.

5. In the Border Cells dialog box, choose a line type in the Line box and choose Grid.

In the following step, you remove lines selectively from the table:

6. In the Line box, choose None, click the vertical lines in the sample table in the Border box to remove them, and choose OK. (This step generally requires a bit of trial and error.)

   Word formats the table with lines under each row.

Edit AUTOEXEC.BAT

When you edit your AUTOEXEC.BAT file in Word, the program word-wraps long lines—a long PATH statement, for example. If you then save AUTOEXEC.BAT with Save As, Word splits the command line as it appears on-screen and creates two lines in the AUTOEXEC.BAT file. The second line is meaningless, of course, since it doesn't contain a command.

To edit and save AUTOEXEC.BAT files that contain long lines, switch to an extremely small point size (1 point, for example), then choose View Zoom and choose a large Zoom size so the text is readable. Choose OK and edit the AUTOEXEC.BAT file. Then save the file in DOS text format with Save As.

Write equations the easy way

When writing equations, you will find it convenient to split the window and display the equation with field codes displayed in one pane and results displayed in the other. Use this technique when you want to edit any field codes and view the results instantly. To open a second pane, drag the split bar or press Alt+- (hyphen) to open the Document Control menu, and then choose Split.

Assign repeated index items to glossaries

When you create an index that contains many repetitions of the same subject heading, you can speed the process of generating the index by assigning that heading to a glossary item. Create the first index entry, select it, and choose Edit Glossary. In the Glossary Name list box, type a name for the index entry and choose Define. To insert the index item at other locations in the document, type the glossary name and press F3.

Format outline headings in Normal or Page Layout mode

You don't have to be in Outline mode to format text as an outline heading. Just stay in Normal or Page Layout view and format the paragraph with a heading style. You also can move the cursor into the heading and press Shift+Alt+left arrow. Word formats the paragraph containing the cursor to the same heading level as the preceding outline heading in the document. You then can press Shift+Alt+left arrow or Shift+Alt+right arrow to adjust the heading to the desired level.

3

CHAPTER

Formatting with Word

Formatting determines the look and style of your document. Word uses four kinds of formatting: character, paragraph, section, and page. You can apply formatting "manually" with individual commands—for example, by pressing Ctrl+B to toggle boldfacing on and off. Or you can assign multiple formatting options to a style that you can apply by choosing it by name from a list or by pressing a shortcut key. You even can assign text and styles to templates to create customized documents—for example, an invoicing template that inserts the text of your letterhead, prompts you to enter the customer's name and billing data, and then inserts the text in the proper locations. As you may expect, with so many formatting options, this chapter is a long one!

Underline text

You can choose from three types of underlining with Word:

- *Single* (underlines words and the space between words)
- *Words only* (underlines words but not spaces)
- *Double* (double-underlines words and spaces)

To underline existing text, select the text and press Ctrl+U for single underlining, Ctrl+W for word underlining, or Ctrl+D for double underlining. To type underlined text, press Ctrl+U, Ctrl+W, or Ctrl+D and begin typing. To turn off the feature, press its invocation key again (Ctrl+U, for example).

Underline subscript and superscript text

To underline subscript and superscript characters without also making the underline a subscript or superscript character, place the text to be underlined in a table cell with a single-line bottom border. Click the cell with the right mouse button to select the cell, then choose Format Border. Choose a line style, then in the Border diagram, click the border that you want to format with the line style. Choose None in the Line area, then click the remaining borders in the Border diagram to format them without lines. Then choose OK.

Fix line spacing for superscript text

Word adds extra space above lines that contain superscript text, resulting in unattractive, inconsistent line spacing. To prevent this problem, follow these steps:

1. Choose Format Style Define and check the Add to Template check box.

2. Choose Paragraph and change the line spacing for the Normal style to Exactly 1 line, choose OK and Change, and choose Close to exit to the editing screen.

3. When you exit the on-screen file, choose Yes when Word asks if you want to make your changes permanent.

With this method, you may need to set line spacing to Auto for text that uses a large font. This is inconvenient, but until Microsoft fixes the problem, it's the only way to correctly format superscript text.

Align superscript and subscript underlines with normal text

A bug in Word prevents underlined superscript and subscript text from aligning correctly with underlined normal text. To work around this limitation, follow these steps to place superscript and subscript characters in an equation field:

1. Press Ctrl+F9 to insert empty field braces. Then type an equation code in the following format:

   {eq \o(2,_)}

   The **\o** code is an overstrike function used to underline superscript or subscript characters. In the example, **(2,_)** tells Word to type a **2** and underline it.

   Note: The equation code does not perform superscript or subscript formatting by itself. To make the characters in the equation field superscript or subscript, continue to follow these steps:

2. Select the equation field by double-clicking one of the braces.

3. Choose Format Character, choose Superscript or Subscript in the Super/subscript text box, and choose OK.

   To underline a longer term, insert multiple underline characters, as in the following example:

   {eq \o(Rev. 222,________)}

If the superscript underlined character doesn't look the same as the underlined character used for surrounding text, you can select the underlined characters in the equation field and change their fonts.

4. To view the results of your work, choose View Field Codes.

Remove optional hyphens

Word's use of hyphens is subtle. You can select three types of hyphens:

Type of Hyphen	Key(s)	Action
Optional hyphen	- (hyphen key)	Remains invisible unless needed at end of line
Nonbreaking hyphen	Shift+Ctrl+-	Prevents hyphenated word from being split at end of line
Nonbreaking space	Shift+Ctrl+space bar	Prevents two words, letters, numbers, for example, from being split at end of line

You can use Word's Replace function to remove optional hyphens from your document. Choose Edit Replace and type ^- (caret, hyphen) in the Find What text box. Make sure that the Replace With text box is empty, and choose Find Next to confirm each replacement. Or choose Replace All to remove all optional hyphens.

Prevent hyphenation

The quickest way to insert hyphens is by choosing Tools Hyphenation after you finish typing a document. You should be aware, however, that Word's hyphenation routine cannot catch unsightly wordwrapped phone numbers and other hyphenated words. To prevent Word from splitting a hyphenated word between lines during automatic hyphenation, press Ctrl+Shift+- (hyphen) to insert nonbreaking hyphens in phone numbers and other words.

Undo hyphenation

After applying automatic hyphenation, you may find that Word has inserted hyphens where you don't want them. To undo hyphenation, you can choose Edit Undo immediately after you hyphenate a document. Or, if you later decide to undo hyphenation, you can use the Replace feature to remove hyphens selectively by following these steps:

1. Choose Edit Replace.
2. In the Find What box, type ^- (caret, hyphen). To insert the caret (^) character, press Shift+6 using the alphanumeric keys. Do not press Ctrl+6.
3. Leave the Replace With box empty, and choose Find Next to confirm each replacement. Or choose Replace All to replace all hyphens without confirmation.
4. If you chose Find Next in step 3, choose Find Next to skip deletion when Word pauses at a hyphen, or choose Replace to delete the hyphen and move on. When you finish deleting hyphens, choose Close.

Add hyphens quickly

The quickest way to hyphenate a document is by choosing Tools Hyphenation and OK.

Cycle through Word's three rulers with the mouse

To cycle through Word's three rulers, click the symbol at the left end of the ruler. (The table ruler only appears when the insertion point is in a table.) The symbols for the three rulers are two triangles, a bracket, and a T (see fig. 3.1).

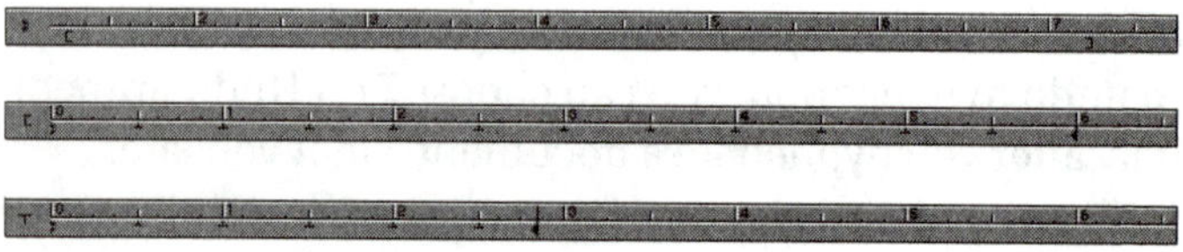

Fig. 3.1 *Word's three rulers.*

You can use the table ruler to work with tables as described in the User's Guide, but it's usually quite frustrating to try to align rows, columns, and cells precisely with the ruler and the mouse. Setting exact measurements in dialog boxes is a much easier and more precise method.

To display table-related dialog boxes quickly, place the insertion point in a table and click the symbol at the left end of the ruler until it becomes a left bracket ([). Double-clicking above the ruler line now displays the Paragraph dialog box, where you can specify alignment of text in table cells. Double-clicking below the ruler line displays the Column Width dialog box, where you can set column widths and spacing between columns. To set widths for all the columns in a table without exiting the dialog box, click the Previous Column and Next Column buttons.

Align tab stops and add tab leaders

You can quickly change the alignment of an existing tab stop or add a tab leader. (A leader—pronounced *leeder*—is a line of dots between tabs.) Double-click the tab stop in the ruler. Word displays the Tabs dialog box with the double-clicked tab selected. Make changes in the Alignment and Leader boxes, choose OK or press Enter, and drag the left margin symbol (the lower triangle at the left end of the tab ruler) back to the left end of the tab ruler.

Create hanging indents

To quickly create a *hanging indent* (the first line of a paragraph is not indented, but subsequent lines are indented), press Shift and drag the bottom half of the left indentation triangle in the ruler. (If you don't press Shift while dragging the bottom half of the triangle, the entire triangle moves, and you set a new left indent.) To quickly create a hanging indent using the existing tab ruler settings, press Ctrl+T (see fig. 3.2).

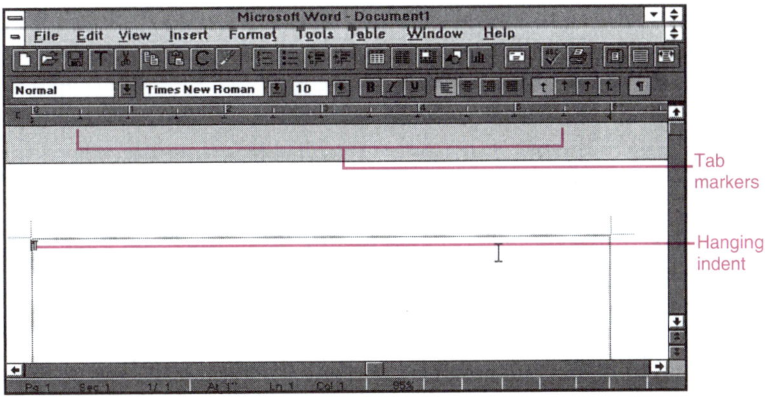

Fig. 3.2 *Hanging indent.*

Use the keyboard to set accurate tabs

It can be difficult to set tabs and margins precisely by dragging symbols on the tab ruler with the mouse. The first line and left indent symbols, in particular, are very small and can be positioned with the mouse only at half-unit intervals on the ruler.

It may seem old-fashioned to set tabs with the Paragraph and Tabs dialog boxes instead of with the mouse and tab ruler, but it's actually faster and more precise. To display the Paragraph dialog box, double-click the number scale above the tab ruler. To display the Tabs dialog box, double-click below the tab ruler or choose Format Paragraph or Format Tabs.

Define tab settings quickly

To quickly define a tab setting (to add leader dots, for example), follow these steps:

1. In the tab ruler, double-click the tab marker you want to define. Word displays the Tabs dialog box.
2. In the Tab Stop Position list box, type **new settings** and choose OK.

Note: When you use this method, Word clears all default tabs to the left of the new tabs. Use this method only to set tabs precisely, when you don't need default tabs.

This method also is a fast way to check the exact position of a tab stop (which is useful for fine work in desktop publishing):

1. Click a paragraph that uses the tab setting.
2. Double-click the tab marker in the ruler.

   Word displays the Tabs dialog box, which shows tab stop positions.

Be careful to click the tab marker, not the surrounding space. If you double-click in the blank space above the ruler, Word displays the Paragraph dialog box; if you double-click in the blank space below the ruler, Word sets a new tab and opens the Tabs dialog box.

Set tabs for selected text

To set tab stops for a given area in a document (a table of figures formatted with tabs, for example), select the area you want to affect and choose Format Tabs.

Solve problems with tabs and unavailable fonts

If Word randomly inserts paragraph marks when you press Tab or tabs don't line up correctly with tabs on the ruler, you probably have used a font that isn't available with the currently installed printer driver.

To find out which fonts are available with your printer, choose File and Print Setup. Then choose a printer and choose Setup. Check the list box for Cartridge or optional fonts. You can choose a cartridge or font set and choose OK twice. Or, to install soft fonts, you can choose Fonts Add fonts and follow the directions.

Fix hanging-indent bugs

When you try to create a hanging indent after you've inserted two page breaks in a document, Word formats the hanging indent incorrectly. To fix this problem, create the page breaks and hanging indent in *exactly* this order:

1. Press Ctrl+Enter to create the first page break. Press Enter immediately after the page break.

2. Press Ctrl+Enter to create the second page break. Create the hanging indent.

You also can fix the problem by using section breaks instead of page breaks. Follow these steps:

1. Choose Insert Break.
2. Choose Next Page and OK.
3. Repeat steps 1 and 2 for the second break.
4. Create the hanging indent.

Add nonbulleted items to bulleted or numbered lists

Sometimes you want to include nonbulleted or non-numbered items in a bulleted or numbered list. To do so, first create the list using a bulleted or numbered paragraph style. Next, go back and add the nonbulleted or non-numbered items. Word will not insert bullets or numbers if you press Enter at the paragraph mark ending a paragraph.

Change bullet or number styles

If you decide to change the style of the bullets or numbers you have used for a list, follow these steps:

1. Select the list and choose Tools Bullets and Numbering.
2. Select the new bullet or number style.
3. Choose Replace Only Bullets or Replace Only Numbers, and choose OK.

Create your own bullets

You can have Word format lists with customized bullets—from happy faces to twisted arrows. To create a new bullet style, follow these steps:

1. Select the list you want to format with bullets.

2. Choose Tools Bullets and Numbering New Bullet.
3. From the Symbols From box, choose a symbol set.
4. Click a symbol and choose OK twice.

If you installed TrueType fonts with Windows 3.1 and higher versions, you will find many decorative symbols in the WingDings symbol set.

Set different margins in the same document

If you format a document with varying margin settings, you must divide the parts of the document that contain different margins into different sections.

You can insert section breaks manually and format the text between the breaks with different margins; or you can choose Format Page Setup and apply margins to the selected text or from the insertion point forward.

Remember that if you delete a section break, you delete the section and lose its margin settings. To restore an accidentally deleted section break, choose Edit Undo before you choose another command; otherwise you will have to create and format the section again. (Save your work frequently!)

Change margins for just a few paragraphs

If you want to change the margins for just one paragraph or a few paragraphs, using indentation shortcut keys is much quicker than using the ruler.

1. Press Ctrl+Shift+F10 to activate the ruler.
2. Use the arrow keys to move the ruler cursor to the position for the indent.

3. Press one of the following keys to set the indent:

Key	Indent
Ctrl+F	First line indent
Ctrl+L	Left indent
Ctrl+M	Left indent moves to preceding tab stop
Ctrl+N	Left indent moves to next tab stop
Ctrl+R	Right indent
Ctrl+T	Hanging indent

Change margins in the middle of a page

Newcomers to Word may have a hard time figuring out how to change margins in the middle of a page. If you simply adjust the margins with the Format Page Setup command, Word doesn't set the new margins at the insertion point but applies those margins to the current page.

To change the margins from the insertion point forward, follow these steps:

1. Choose Insert Break. The Section Break dialog box appears. Choose Continuous and OK.
2. Move the insertion point below the new section break and choose Format Section Layout. The Section Start dialog box appears. Choose Continuous and OK.
3. Choose Page Setup, select the Margins button (if it isn't already selected), and set the new margins.
4. Choose This Point Forward from the Apply To box and choose OK.

To indent only a few paragraphs, it's simpler to select the paragraphs and choose the Format Paragraph command.

Set margins for text in a frame

To set margins for text in a frame, follow these steps:

1. Click the frame border to select the frame.
2. Choose Format Paragraph.
3. Set left, right, and first line margins for the frame text.
4. To insert space between the top and bottom of the frame text and the frame borders, specify measurements for Before and After in the Spacing box.
5. Choose OK.

Create a table of figures or references quickly

To create a table of figures or references quickly, assign an unused outline heading level (for example, Heading 9) to the figure descriptions or references. When you choose Insert Table of Contents to generate the table, specify that you want to generate a table using only Heading 9.

Add space between headers or footers and document text

To add extra space between headers or footers and the main text of a document, in the header window, press Enter after the header text or before the footer text. Word adjusts the top or bottom margins of the main body text accordingly. (Remember, the new "margin settings" don't appear in the Format Page Setup dialog box or in File Print Preview.)

Print headers/footers

You can create headers/footers that display the total number of pages in a document (Page 12 of 38, for example). The following example refers to headers but the steps also apply to footers.

Create a header or footer as you normally would, and perform the following steps:

1. In the header editing screen, type **Page** and press Alt+Shift+P to insert a page-numbering code.
2. Type **of** and choose Insert Field. Choose No. of pages in the Insert Field Type list box, and choose OK. To update the field codes in the header at any time, press F9.

To see the numeric result of all the field codes in a document, change to Page Layout mode (choose View Page Layout), then press Shift+F9.

To update the field, place the cursor in the field and press F9. If Word beeps, it means the field is locked. To unlock the field, place the cursor in the field and press Alt+Shift+F11.

To have Word update all fields when you print a document, choose Tools Options, press P to display Print options, mark the Update Fields check box, then choose OK.

Insert a page break in justified text

When you insert a page break in justified text, Word justifies the line before the page break. If there are just a few words in the line, this results in unusually wide word spacing in the line. To avoid this problem, press Enter before you create a hard page break.

Insert multiple copies of the same symbol

To insert multiple copies of a Word symbol (for example, a copyright symbol or special type of bullet), you don't have to choose Insert Symbol each time. Instead, follow these steps:

1. Choose Insert Symbol, choose a symbol set from the Symbols From list, and double-click the symbol you want.

   Word returns to the editing screen and inserts the symbol.

2. Before you press another key, move the cursor to the next location where you want to insert a symbol and press F4 (the Repeat key) to insert another copy of the symbol. Repeat at each location where you need a symbol.

Another method to insert multiple copies of a Word symbol follows:

1. Follow step 1 in the preceding procedure.
2. Turn on field code display (choose View Field Codes).
3. Select the symbol field.

   To select a symbol field with the mouse, double-click one of its curly braces ({}).

4. Press Ctrl+C to copy the symbol to the Clipboard.
5. Move the cursor to the next location where you want to insert a symbol, and press Ctrl+V to insert a symbol.

Unlike using the Repeat key (F4), using Paste (Ctrl+V) enables you to edit text between insertions, as long as you don't cut or paste other text to the Clipboard, which replaces the Clipboard contents.

Create a symbol library

If you use decorative fonts frequently (Wingdings, Zapf Dingbats, and so on), you may find it easier to insert these special characters by copying them from a customized symbol library than by using the Insert Symbol command.

The Insert Symbol screen displays characters in almost unreadable size, making it hard to find the symbols you need, even though clicking a symbol displays it in a larger size. In a symbol library, you can format the symbol characters in any size.

To create a symbol library, follow these steps:

1. Choose a large character size. Click the point size list in the ribbon, or choose Format Character, choose a large size in the Points list, and choose OK.
2. Choose Insert Symbol.
3. In the Symbols From box, choose a decorative font.
4. Hold down the left mouse button while you move the mouse pointer from left to right along each row, displaying the symbols in an enlarged window.
5. Choose OK to insert a copy of a symbol.
6. Repeat steps 2 through 5 for each symbol that you regularly use.
7. Save the symbol library in its own file.
8. When you need to use symbols, open the symbol library file in a second window and copy symbols into your document.

Use macros to insert frequently used symbols

You can assign special symbols to macro shortcut keys by following these steps:

1. Choose Tools Record Macro.
2. Type a name and choose a shortcut key, and then choose OK.
3. Choose Insert Symbol.
4. In the Symbols From box, choose a decorative font.
5. Hold down the left mouse button while you move the mouse pointer from left to right along each row, displaying the symbols in an enlarged window.
6. Press OK to insert a copy of a symbol.
7. Choose Tools Stop Recorder.

When you press the macro's shortcut key, Word inserts the symbol.

Use Shift+F3 to change uppercase and lowercase quickly

To change lowercase or uppercase and lowercase text to all caps, select the text and press Shift+F3. You can change lowercase text quickly to uppercase and lowercase text by selecting the text and pressing Shift+F3 twice. To return the text to all lowercase, press Shift+F3 again. You can restore normal sentence capitalization (initial capital letter) by choosing Edit Undo (or pressing Ctrl+Z).

Change Word's formatting defaults

If you frequently change Word's default formatting settings, you can save time by changing the defaults permanently. To begin, change the default page margins. Choose Format Page Setup. Make your changes, and choose the Set Default button. Choose OK.

To set other formatting defaults, follow these steps:

1. Open a document using the NORMAL template. Choose Format Style Define, and select the Add to Template check box.
2. Make your changes to font, spacing, and other settings and choose OK.

When you exit the on-screen file, choose Yes at the prompt to save global changes.

Copy character formatting quickly

After you apply character formatting, you can quickly apply the same formatting to other text. You also can type similarly formatted text elsewhere in the document. Follow these steps:

1. Choose Format Character, choose your character formatting options, and choose OK.
2. Type text in the new format. Select the text to which you want to apply the same format and press F4.

Word applies the character formatting you chose in step 1.

Follow these steps to copy formatting from existing text to other text using the mouse:

1. Select the text you want to format. Position the mouse pointer in text that has the format you want to copy.
2. Press Ctrl+Shift and click the mouse button.

If you accidentally move the insertion point twice instead of immediately reapplying formatting, you still can copy the formatting. Choose Edit Repeat Formatting.

Copy multiple formats

To copy multiple formats (for example, a Times Roman 24-point bold italic font), choose Format Character to apply formatting instead of using the character-formatting tools in the ruler. If you use the ruler, Word copies only the format that was assigned last.

Remove all document formatting

If you have made a mess of part or all of a document and want to start over, you can remove all formatting from selected text or from the entire document. Follow these steps:

1. With the document displayed on-screen, choose File Save As.
2. In the Save File as Type box, choose DOS Text (*.tx8). If you choose DOS Text w/line breaks (*.tx8), Word inserts a paragraph mark after each line. If you choose Text Only (*.txt), Word retains field codes but converts field braces and codes to text.
3. Type a name in the File Name box and choose OK.

To retrieve the file, follow these steps:

1. Close or exit the file on-screen. Choose File Open.
2. Type the exported file's name and choose OK.
3. In the Convert File dialog box, choose DOS Text and choose OK.

Word retrieves the unformatted file.

Work with sections

You can copy, move, and delete section marks. If you double-click a section mark, Word displays the Section

Layout dialog box. This dialog box is very useful when you want to set new margins in the middle of a page, or if you want to add line numbering to a section.

To make quick work of inserting sections, copy a formatted section mark to a glossary item. You then can quickly insert it into other documents that need the same section formatting. Follow these steps:

1. Format a section. Choose Insert Break, choose a section break type, and choose OK.
2. Select the section mark (a grayed double line) and choose Edit Glossary, type a name, and choose Define.
3. To insert section formatting, choose Edit Glossary, choose the section mark by name, and choose Insert.

   Word inserts the section mark.

Before you insert a section break, apply all consistent section formatting first. That way, you won't need to apply so much formatting manually in other sections.

If you accidentally delete a section mark, you delete all the section formatting that precedes that mark. To restore the mark, before you do anything else, choose Edit Undo (Ctrl+Z).

Format sections without page numbers

Follow these steps to format selected sections of a document without page numbers:

1. Move the cursor into the section for which you want to omit page numbers. Choose View Normal.
2. Choose View Header/Footer, choose a header or footer, and choose OK.

3. In the Header/Footer pane, select the page number and press Del.
4. If the header or footer contains no other text than a page number, press the space bar and choose Close. If the header/footer contains other text, delete the page number and choose Close.

Word omits page numbering for the current section and all other sections that follow. To restore page numbering to subsequent sections, follow these steps:

1. Move the cursor into the next section and choose View Header/Footer. Choose a header or footer and choose OK.
2. In the Header or Footer pane, choose the # button to insert a page number. Choose Close.

Word restores page numbers to the current section and subsequent sections.

Create long headings above columnar text

To insert a long title horizontally across the page above several columns of body text, insert a continuous section break before and after the title. Then format the title as single-column text.

To insert a continuous section break, follow these steps:

1. Choose Insert Break.
2. In the Section Break box, choose Continuous.
3. Place the cursor after the title and repeat steps 1 and 2.
4. Choose OK.

To format a title as single-column text, follow these steps:

1. Select the title.
2. Choose Format Columns.
3. In the Number of Columns box, choose 1 and then choose OK.

Format part of a page in columns

The User's Guide is vague about formatting text in columns without changing other text on the same page. Follow these steps:

1. Move the insertion point to the end of the text that you want to format in columns.
2. Choose Insert Break.
3. In the Section Break box, choose Continuous. Then choose OK.
4. Move the insertion point to the start of the text and repeat steps 2 through 3 to insert another section break.
5. Select the text you want to format and choose Format Columns.
6. Enter the new column specifications.
7. From the Apply To box, choose Selected Sections, and then choose OK.

Word formats only the text in the section you just created.

Prevent widow and orphan headings

You're fighting a rush deadline and print the final—you hope—draft of a report. To your dismay, you find that a section heading has been printed at the bottom of a page, separated from its text which falls at the top of the next page. To prevent this disaster, change the heading style by following these steps:

1. Choose Format Style and select a style in the Style Name dialog box.
2. Choose Define Paragraph.
3. In the Pagination box, select Keep with Next. Then choose OK, Change, Yes (if you're changing a standard style), and Close.

Now Word will never strand a heading at the bottom of a page. If you want a heading style to always land at the top of a page, repeat the process, but in step 3, choose Page Break Before in the Pagination box.

Check page layout quickly

For a quick view of the current page that closely approximates the final, printed version, in Page Layout view, click the Zoom Whole Page button, which is the third button from the right end of the toolbar. This is quicker than using Print Preview or Zoom.

In Zoom Whole Page mode, you can perform normal editing functions such as cutting and pasting, which are not supported in Print Preview. To switch back to normal page view, click the Page Width button at the far right end of the toolbar.

Create shadowed check boxes

The Word User's Guide recommends that you create shadowed check boxes with Microsoft Draw. If you have installed the TrueType fonts supplied with Windows 3.1 and later versions, an easier way exists. Follow these steps:

1. Move the cursor where you want to insert a symbol, then choose Insert Symbol. In the Symbols From box, select the Wingdings character set.

In the center of the third row from the top, you find four check boxes. The third check box from the left is shadowed below, and the fourth is shadowed above.

2. To display an enlarged view of a check box, click it and hold down the mouse button.

3. To insert a check box, double-click it or select it and choose OK.

You can enlarge or reduce a check box in one of three ways:

- Select the check box and change the font size with the ribbon.
- Choose Format Character, select a font size, and choose OK.
- Select the check box and press Ctrl+F2 to enlarge it or Ctrl+Shift+F2 to reduce it.

If you use many check boxes, you can assign each size and design to a glossary item by following these steps:

1. Select a check box and choose Edit Glossary.

2. Type a glossary name (for example, **Box1**) and choose Define.

To insert a check box, type the glossary name and press F3. Word deletes the name and inserts a check box.

Create an em-dash

To create an *em-dash* (a long dash), turn on NumLock and press Alt while you type **0150** from the number pad. When you release Alt, the em-dash appears on-screen.

Sort a numbered, lettered, or bulleted list

After you create a list, you may want to apply bullets, numbers, or letters to the list, and then sort the list items. Select the list and choose Tools Sorting. Choose Ascending or Descending and choose OK.

If you have applied bullets, numbers, or letters to a list, you can sort the list in two ways. If the list is bulleted, you need to sort the list only on the second field (the first word of each item in the list). Choose Tools Sorting, Ascending or Descending. In the Sorting dialog box, choose the Tab button, in the Field Number box type **2**, and then choose OK.

If the list is lettered or numbered, remove the letters or numbers and then sort the list and reapply numbering. Or sort the list on field 2, and then tell Word to reapply numbering.

To renumber a list, select the list and choose Tools Bullets and Numbering, choose the Numbered List button, choose a Format, Separator, and Start At option, and then choose OK. When Word asks if you want to replace existing bullets with numbers, choose Yes.

4

CHAPTER

Using the Spelling and Grammar Checkers

Word's spelling and grammar checkers cannot teach you to write like Shakespeare, but they can help you avoid embarrassing errors. As you use the grammar checker, you become aware of ways to write with greater clarity and precision. As you eliminate certain errors from your writing, you can save time by telling the grammar checker not to look for those mistakes.

Be wary of placing too much trust in the spelling checker. It can overlook such simple errors as *to* used in place of *too* or *two*.

Make editing changes during a spell check

During a spell-checking session, you can switch to the document text to make editing changes. Click in the document or press Ctrl+Tab to activate the document window. (If the Spelling dialog box is in the way, drag it to a new location.) After editing, choose **S**tart from the Spelling dialog box to continue checking spelling.

Check grammar but not spelling

When you perform a grammar check with Word 2.0 and later versions, Word also performs a spell check by default. If you don't want the grammar checker to check spelling, you can turn off this option by following these steps:

1. Choose T**o**ols **O**ptions, and press G twice to choose the Grammar options.
2. Choose C**u**stomize Settings, and in the Grammar list box, clear the Spelling Errors check box. Then choose OK twice.

Spell-check a single word

If you are not sure how to spell a single word, move the insertion point to the word and press F7. If the word is spelled correctly, Word displays a message to that effect; if not, it displays the Spelling dialog box and tries to display a correct spelling. You can use one of the alternative spellings that Word displays, or you can click the name of a custom dictionary, and then click Add. This is a great way to build a custom dictionary as you type.

Spell-check technical documents

Spell-checking documents that contain parts lists, technical data, and other sections containing alphanumeric codes, can be extremely annoying. To skip "words" that combine numbers and letters, click **O**ptions in the Spelling dialog box, on the Tools menu, and then check Words with Numbers in the Ignore box. You also can tell Word to skip technical material by selecting lists and tables as you type them and giving them No Proofing status. To do so, select the text and choose Format Language (no proofing) and OK. Word ignores the text during a spelling session.

Use the grammar checker selectively

You may not need all the information that the grammar checker provides, but you may find it very useful to correct specific errors that you tend to make—for example, redundant expressions. To perform a customized grammar check, choose Tools Grammar, wait for the grammar checker to stop and make a suggestion, and choose Options Customize Settings. In the dialog box, choose rules for business writing or for casual writing, deselect all the grammar and style options (except Redundant Expressions), and choose OK twice. Choose Next Sentence to continue checking grammar.

Use the grammar checker for more complete spell-checking

A notorious deficiency of spelling checkers is their inability to spot improper word use: *two* for *too* or *to*, *their* for *there*, *four* for *for*, and so on. The grammar checker usually can detect these errors; therefore, it's a good idea to perform a grammar check after spell-checking a document. To speed the process, customize the grammar checker as described in the preceding tip, but in the Customize Grammar Settings dialog box, choose Misused Words in the Style box.

5

CHAPTER

Managing Word for Windows Files

Document management involves finding, moving, copying, deleting, and displaying Word for Windows document files and graphics, spreadsheet, and database files.

Word provides excellent document-management tools through its **Find File** command. To open the Find File dialog box, choose **File Find File**. In the Find File dialog box, you can search for files by name, type, location, document summary information, and creation date. You then can sort the listed files; display them with selected information; and open, print, delete, or copy files. You even can use a preview box to view the contents of files that contain text and/or graphic images.

This chapter gives tips for using **Find File** and other document management functions of Microsoft Windows and Microsoft Word.

Use file names that sort correctly

To quickly save and identify several versions of the same file, give the files sequential numbers: SALES01, SALES02, and so on. Be sure to include a 0 in single-digit numbers, so Word places these files ahead of file names with double-digit numbers in its sorted file name lists. (SALES11 would appear before SALES5, for example.)

Track document drafts

Do you and your co-workers pass around draft revisions of reports and other documents in hard copy? In the rush of deadlines, versions can get switched. To ensure that you're working with the latest version, you can format a header as hidden text, and then print drafts with hidden text displayed. Follow these steps:

1. To create hidden text in a header, format the header as you normally would (choose **V**iew **H**eader/Footer, then choose Header or Footer, then OK); choose Forma**t** **C**haracter, select the **H**idden check box, and choose OK before you begin typing.

2. In the header, place fields that print the writer's name, time and date printed, comments, total editing time, and so on.

   Word displays hidden text with a dotted underline. To turn on the display of hidden text, make sure you are in Page Layout view (choose **V**iew **P**age Layout). Click the paragraph mark at the right end of the ribbon. Or, to make the display of hidden text the default, choose T**o**ols **O**ptions, type **v** to display View options, and select Hi**d**den Text in the Nonprinting Characters box.

3. To insert fields, choose **I**nsert Fiel**d**, select a field in the Insert **F**ield Type box, and choose OK.

Word doesn't display hidden text in the Print Preview screen. To print a document with hidden text, follow these steps:

1. Choose **File Print** and set any desired options in the dialog box.
2. Choose **Options** and select the **Hidden Text** check box. Then choose OK twice.

Convert Word for the Mac graphics to Word for Windows

You will find it a very slow process to convert Macintosh Word files that contain PICT and PNT graphics if you let Word for Windows perform the conversions. To speed the process, do the conversions on the Mac. In Word for the Mac, choose **File Save As**. Type a file name, choose Word for Windows 2.0 in the Save File as **Type** list box, and then choose **Save**. Copy the file onto an IBM disk for transfer, and you should be able to read the file in Word for Windows with no problems.

Insert document summary comments in document text

To edit the text of summary comments, you normally choose **File Summary Info** and make changes in the **Comments** text box.

To insert the contents of the Comments box in a document, follow these steps:

1. Position the cursor where you want to insert comments.
2. Choose **Insert Field**.
3. Choose **Comments** in the **Insert Field Type** list, and choose OK.

Word inserts the contents of the Comments box in the Summary Info dialog box into the document.

You can append text to the Comments box without opening the Summary Info dialog box by following these steps:

1. Follow steps 1–3 from the preceding list to insert a Comments field code.
2. If the field code display is turned off, choose **View Field Codes**. Word displays the comments field:

   ```
   {comments }
   ```

   Note: The extra space is not a typo.
3. Move the cursor to the left of the right field bracket and type a double quote. Then press Ctrl+F9 to insert a nested field.
4. Type the text you want to append to the summary information by using the following format:

   ```
   {comments "{comments} this is the added comment"}
   ```
5. Before moving the cursor outside of the field, press F9 to update the field.
6. To verify that Word has appended your changes to the document summary, choose **File Summary Info** and view the contents of the Comments box.

   Note: Summary Info comments are limited to 255 characters.

Turn off summary information

If you rarely need to fill in summary information for a file, you can tell Word not to prompt you for summary information. Follow these steps:

1. Choose Tools Options, type **s** to display Save options, and deselect the Prompt for Summary Info check box.

   So far, so good; but what happens when you *do* want to store summary information with a file?

2. When you save the file, choose File Save As Options, check the Prompt for Summary Info check box, and choose OK twice.

Word displays the Summary Info dialog box for this file only.

Conserve disk space

When disk space is scarce (for example, when you're transferring big files on floppies), you can save room by switching from Fast Save to Normal Save. You also don't have to change the default Fast Save setting for just one document. Instead, to save the file, choose File Save As Options, deselect the Allow Fast Saves check box, and click OK twice. This action changes the setting for future Word sessions.

Open the Find File dialog box

You can open the Find File dialog box in three ways:

- Choose File Find File.
- Choose File Open Find File.
- Choose Insert File or Picture, and choose Find File.

Although you can open graphics files by choosing File Find File or Insert File, using Insert Picture provides a complete list of graphics file conversions in the List Files of Type list box. You then can choose a graphics file type to instantly display a list of available files of that type.

Similarly, choosing Insert File enables you to choose document file conversion filters from the List Files of Type list box.

Work around a frustrating Find File bug

You know the file you're looking for with Find File contains the words "Joe DiMaggio," yet Word doesn't locate the file. Word can't find the file because the Find File command ignores files saved with Fast Saves turned on when you specify search text in the Any Text box in the Search dialog box. To make your full-text searches work, you must turn off Fast Saves. Choose Tools **O**ptions, type **s** to display Save options, and clear the Allow **F**ast Saves check box.

Fine-tune Find File searches

For quicker searching with the Find File command, narrow your searches. Searching for *for* locates files that contain the words *foreign, fork, ford,* and so on. To locate the word *for,* type the search text in quotes, followed by a space: **"for"** .

Always enclose search text in quotes if it contains spaces or punctuation. Be aware that Word interprets the ampersand (&) as a *logical* "and." If you try to search for "Mutt & Jeff," Word locates files that contain both words, but not necessarily the phrase "Mutt & Jeff."

Word displays a cryptic `Find File` error message

When you try to delete a file with Find File, Word may display a cryptic `file in use` message, even though the file isn't open. What has probably happened is that you have cut or copied text from the file during the current working session. To delete the file, you must first quit and then reload the Word program.

The screen that Word displays if you choose Help at the error message dialog box doesn't mention this method.

Change the DOC default file name extension

You can change the DOC extension that Word automatically assigns to document file names. This capability may be useful for naming the files for a specific project or to avoid confusing Word documents with other programs' DOC files. To change the DOC extension, follow these steps:

1. Choose **F**ile **O**pen, type **\windows\win.ini** in the File **N**ame list box, and choose OK.
2. Find the [Microsoft Word 2.0] section of the WIN.INI file.
3. Look for a line that reads:

   ```
   DOC-EXTENSION=DOC
   ```

4. To change the default extension to RPT, erase the DOC extension and type **RPT** in its place:

   ```
   DOC-EXTENSION=RPT
   ```

   If your WIN.INI file doesn't have a DOC-EXTENSION line, move to the end of the [Microsoft Word 2.0] section and type the extension on its own line:

   DOC-EXTENSION=RPT

This next step is very important. You *MUST* save the WIN.INI file in ASCII format. If you save it as a Word document, you can't load Windows. To save WIN.INI, follow these steps:

1. Choose **F**ile Save **A**s
2. In the Save File as **T**ype list box, choose Text Only (*.txt), then choose OK.

To activate the new default, you need to exit and reload Windows.

Locate files by type

Word can search an entire drive and list all files of a specified type; for example, BMP or PCX graphics files. To locate files by type, follow these steps:

1. Choose File Find File, and choose Search.
2. Type ***.bmp** as the file name, choose the C drive in the Drives box, and click Create New List in the Options box.
3. Choose Start Search.

You can preview graphics files without leaving the Find File dialog box. Follow these steps:

1. In the Find File dialog box, Choose Options Content and choose OK.
2. Select a file in the File Name list and choose Preview to display the image in the Content pane, and then choose Close.
3. When you find the image you want to use, choose Insert Picture to retrieve the image into the active document.

Reopen a file automatically to resume working

You can tell Word to automatically reopen the file you were working on before you last exited the program. Follow these steps:

1. From the Windows Program Manager, choose the Word for Windows icon.

To choose the Word icon, click it once or highlight it with the arrow keys.

2. Choose **F**ile **P**roperties.
3. After the name of the Word EXE program file, type the characters **/mFile1**, without adding a space before the slash. For example, type:

   c:\winword\word.exe/mFile1

   This command tells Word to automatically load file number one at the bottom of the File menu, which is the file you last edited.

   You also can tell Word not to open any file when you run the program—not even a new file. To accomplish this task, follow steps 1–3 but after the .EXE file name, type **/n**:

   c:\winword\word.exe/n

When you load Word, it no longer opens a new file named Document1.

Open files quickly

When you choose **F**ile **O**pen, you don't have to move through the File Name list box with the mouse or with the arrow keys. Instead, type the first few letters of the file you want to open and press the down arrow. The cursor moves directly to the specified file name.

Create master documents easily

You can create master documents in two ways: with INCLUDE fields or RD (Read Document) fields. Of the two methods, RD is the least time-consuming.

INCLUDE generates one very long file in the process of compiling tables of contents, indexes, and lists, whereas RD pulls information from one file at a time.

To use RD, create a master document file with an RD field for each of the constituent files. For each file, type **RD** (or **rd**) and the file name. For example, type:

rd chapter1.doc
rd chapter2.doc
rd chapter3.doc
rd chapter4.doc

To generate a table of contents, index, or list, position the cursor at the position in the master document where you want the table to be inserted, and generate as usual.

Add a File Delete menu item

Deleting a file in Word involves many steps: choose File Find File Search, type a file spec and path, choose Start Search, highlight the file name, and choose Delete Yes. A macro makes deleting files much quicker.

Follow these steps to create a delete files macro:

1. Choose Tools Macro, type a name for the macro, and choose Edit.
2. In the macro editor, type the macro exactly as shown:

```
Sub MAIN
Input "Delete:" ; fil$
If(len(fil$) > 0) Then Kill fil$
End Sub
```

3. Choose File Close and choose Yes at the prompt to save changes.

To run the macro, follow these steps:

1. Choose Tools Macro, choose the macro by name from the list box, and choose Run.

   Word displays `Delete?` in the status bar.

2. Type a file name, including a path if the file isn't in the current directory, and press Enter.

Word deletes the file and returns you to the editing window. If the file doesn't exist or isn't in the current directory, Word displays a `File not found` message in a dialog box. Choose OK to return to the editing screen.

You can use DOS wild cards such as *.DOC. or SMITH??.DOC to delete multiple files, but be careful. Word does not ask you to confirm the deletion of each file; therefore, to delete multiple files, it's usually safer to take the time to use File Find File.

You can assign the delete file macro to a shortcut key or an item on the File menu. To create a menu item, follow these steps:

1. Choose Tools Options and press M to display the Menu options.
2. Choose the Macros button in the Show box and the Global button in the Context box.
3. Choose the macro by name from the Macros list box.
4. Choose &File in the Menu box.
5. Choose Add Close.

Word adds the macro's name to the File menu. To delete a file, you now can choose File and press the underlined letter in the macro's name. If the underlined letter duplicates another underlined letter in the File menu, press the letter repeatedly until the file deletion item is highlighted and press Enter.

You also can rename the macro to avoid duplicating another menu item's underlined keys. Follow these steps:

1. Choose Tools Macro.
2. Highlight the macro's name, choose Rename, and type a new name.
3. Choose OK and Close.

To assign the macro to a shortcut key, follow these steps:

1. Choose Tools Options and press K to display the keyboard layout screen.
2. Choose the Macros button in the Show box and the Global button in the Context box.
3. Highlight the file deletion macro by name in the Macros box.
4. Select a shortcut key in the Shortcut Key box and choose Add Close.

You now can run the macro by pressing its shortcut key.

Use Word to create hypertext reference documents

You can easily format Word documents for convenient use as complex reference works—for example, to create a company-wide employee directory.

The best tool for organizing many types of long reference documents is Word's outline function. In fact, Hewlett-Packard uses an outlining program, Symantec's GrandView, in its technical support center to quickly look up answers to technical questions.

You also can create "hypertext" buttons (called *Go To Buttons*) that, when clicked with the mouse, move the insertion point immediately to the location designated by the button. The process of organizing documents with Go To buttons, however, is much more complicated than using the outline feature and, therefore, should be used judiciously.

Documents formatted with Go To buttons may need to be carefully updated each time you make editing changes that change the order and location of information. Before automating documents with Go To buttons, you must first gather related information at the same location. This task may involve many hours of effort, depending on the length and complexity of the information.

Despite these complexities, Go To buttons do have appropriate applications for which they can be used with a minimum of effort.

To see how Go To buttons work, retrieve the file named CONVINFO.DOC, supplied with Word. This file includes Go To buttons that you can click in order to move to corresponding sections of the text.

Preparing documents for information retrieval with the outline function is easier than the preceding. You still must group related information, but you can group it more loosely. Just move or copy related sections under adjacent subheadings:

```
Coronary Bypass Survival Statistics
Open Heart Surgery Review Board Statement
Projected Patient Loads for Coronary IC 1993
```

Next, place related subheadings under general subject headings:

```
CORONARY SURGERY
Coronary Bypass Survival Statistics
Projected Patient Loads for Coronary IC 1993
Open Heart Surgery Review Board Statement
```

To locate specific information, collapse the document outline and search the hierarchical outline heading structure, expanding those headings that contain relevant data.

It isn't within the scope of this book to give a tutorial on formatting documents as outlines; however, since Go To buttons have some very useful applications that can be covered quickly, this book will provide tips for creating hypertext documents in Word. You can place Go To buttons, for example, at the top of product catalogs, instruction manuals, phone directories, and other simple reference works to enable readers to jump to appropriate sections with mouse clicks.

To create a Go To button, follow these steps:

1. Choose **Insert Field**, choose Go To button in the Insert Field **Type** list box, and choose OK.

   Word inserts a {gotobutton} field code in the document screen. If you don't see the code, choose **View Field Codes** to turn on the display of hidden field codes.

2. Using Word's editing keys, type a Go To button name inside the field brackets after gotobutton. After the name, type the text that users will see displayed in the editing screen, and that they can double-click to activate the button. For example:

```
{gotobutton parts "Click here to jump to the parts list."}
```

3. Insert a bookmark at the destination for the Go To button. To insert a bookmark, move the cursor to the location you want to jump to, and then choose **Insert Bookmark**, type a bookmark name (for example, **parts**), and choose OK.

Notice that bookmarks aren't displayed in any of Word's screen views. To rename or delete a bookmark, you must use the bookmark dialog box (choose Insert Bookmark).

Go To buttons are inactive with field codes displayed. Before you can test the button, therefore, you need to turn off the field codes display: choose View Field Codes.

Double-clicking the message `Click here to jump to the parts list.` now takes you to the corresponding bookmark. To return to a Goto button, press Shift+F5 before you use any editing keys.

If you routinely edit text before returning to a Go To button, you may find it convenient to create a second Go To button and bookmark that return you to the location of the first Go To button.

Create decorative Go To buttons

The Goto buttons in several documents supplied with Word, including CONVINFO.DOC, were formatted with Microsoft Draw. To create Goto buttons with similar graphic effects, follow these steps:

1. Insert a Goto button as described earlier.
2. Turn field codes on (choose View Field Codes).
3. Move the cursor into the message area of the Go To button code, choose Insert Object Microsoft Drawing from the Object Type list box, and choose OK.
4. Create the graphic button in Microsoft Draw, using text and shading functions.

To create shading, follow these steps:

1. Choose the Microsoft Draw box tool.
2. Choose Draw Framed to create a borderless box.

3. Draw the box.
4. Use the arrow tool to select the group of objects (lines, text, and shading) you just created.

   This action groups the objects so they can be moved and saved as one object.
5. Choose File Exit and Return.

Word displays an MS Draw object code in the Go To button field. To use the button, choose View Field Codes and double-click the button. To make changes to the shaded button in Microsoft Draw, move the insertion point onto the button and choose Edit Microsoft Drawing Object.

6

CHAPTER

Printing Tips and Tricks

A long time ago, when microcomputers were first invented, setting up and using a printer could be a big headache because you had to install your printer for each program you used. With Microsoft Windows, you only have to install a printer from the large list of supported makes and models, and then forget about it. Any new Windows applications you acquire can use the Windows printer drivers you have already installed. Many ways still exist, however, to customize your printing with Windows programs such as Microsoft Word.

Create watermarks

You can tell Word to print a *watermark* (text that prints over the body text of a document) in a large font over the regular text on the page.

If you own a PostScript printer, try using the WaterMark macro supplied with Word. This macro automates the process and is described in the text file named NEWMACRO.DOC that also comes with Word.

If you own any other type of printer, you must put the watermark text in a header or footer. The trick to make

Word print a header or footer over the other text on the page is to specify a minus quantity for the top margin (if you're using a header) or for the bottom margin (if you're using a footer).

Before you change the margin setting, first create the watermark text in a header using WordArt or a regular font. Follow these steps:

1. Choose View Header/Footer.
2. Choose Header or Footer and choose OK.
3. In the Header or Footer pane, create the text using any fonts available for your printer.

   You can use WordArt in the header or footer pane for special effects, as described later.
4. Choose Close to exit the header or footer pane.

The reason for creating the watermark text before setting the margins is that if you set the margins first, Word doesn't display the header text in the editing screen. After creating the header text, you must choose Page Layout view in order to see the text on your monitor.

To create the watermark text with WordArt, follow these steps:

1. Choose Insert Object MS WordArt and choose OK.
2. In WordArt, create the text and choose OK.

   For details on using WordArt, consult the Word User's Guide or Que's *Using Word for Windows 2.*

   To preserve the readability of the underlying document text, consider using a white fill or light gray shading for the watermark.
3. To resize the WordArt object, select the object by clicking on it, and drag the handles.

You also can create watermark text by creating a Picture or Drawing. Follow these steps to set the negative margin:

1. Choose Format Page Setup Margins.
2. Set Top or Bottom to -1" for a 1" margin, and then choose OK.

After setting the minus margin, you probably will not be able to see all of the watermark—even in Page Layout view. It will print, however, in the position you specified before you changed the margin.

Note that this tip applies only to Word 2.x and later versions. With Word 1.x, you must choose Format Document to specify a minus quantity for the margin. Because Word 1.x doesn't include WordArt, you have to use a separate graphics program to create watermarks by using special effects, such as rotated text.

Use dot-matrix printers for better print quality

You may find that the print quality of dot-matrix text printed with Word is poorer than you get with your DOS applications—especially in landscape mode. To remedy this problem, try installing the C and D fonts provided with Windows for use with dot-matrix printers. From the Program Manager, Open the Main group and run the Control Panel. Choose Fonts and install the C and D fonts.

Change print options

Word enables you to change certain print options (such as document size and paper source) by using the Print Setup dialog box or the Page Setup dialog box. The changes you make with File Print Setup apply to all documents you print after making changes. Changes you make with Format Page Setup apply only to the current document and override any default settings.

Print letterhead pages quickly

Many single-bin laser printers, such as the HP LaserJet Series III, give first priority to a single page that you slide into the manual tray as far as it goes—even if you have set the printer to print from the bin. You, therefore, don't have to set your printer to manual feed mode or load letterhead in the paper bin to print a first page on letterhead.

Work with another program while printing

When you start a print job, you have to wait momentarily while Word sends the file(s) to the Windows print spooler. You can avoid this brief delay by pressing Alt+Tab to switch to the Program Manager and run another program. This action doesn't always work, however, but you can always switch to Program Manager if you reduce the size of the Word window before printing. You then can click in the underlying Program Manager window.

Change priority setting to speed up printing

Word documents print faster with Print Manager if you change the priority setting for print jobs. (The default Windows installation sets Print manager for Medium Priority.) Follow these steps:

1. Press Alt+Esc to switch to Program Manager.
2. Open the Main group and run Print Manager.
3. Choose Options High Priority, then close Print Manager and the Main group.
4. Press Alt+Esc to switch back to Word.

Word now prints faster, but Word commands may run a bit slower while documents are printing.

Change the default address position for the envelope feature

You can change the position where Word prints the recipient's address when you use the Create Envelope feature. You can drag the address to a new position or specify the exact position. To specify the exact position, follow these steps:

1. Choose File New, choose a template in the Use Template list, and choose OK.
2. Choose Tools Create Envelope Add to Document.
3. Choose Format Style and in the Style Name box, choose `envelope address`.
4. Choose Define Frame and type an exact measurement in the Position box.

   The number you type in the Position box is the distance from the left margin, which by default is 2 inches from the left edge of the envelope. Typing **1.5"** in the Position box, therefore, will print the address 2" + 1.5" – 3.5" from the left edge.
5. In the Relative To box, choose Page.
6. In the Distance from Text box, choose .1".

   The Distance From Text setting tells Word how much white space to leave between the address and any nearby text. Because the address is positioned a safe distance from other text, this setting is unimportant and can be set to any small value such as .1".
7. In the Vertical box, type an exact measurement in the Position box—for example, type **1.75** for a #10 business envelope.
8. In the Relative To box, choose Page and choose 0" in the Distance from Text box.

9. Choose OK and choose Apply Yes.

You also can use the mouse to drag the address frame to a new position. Follow these steps:

1. Choose View Page Layout.
2. Choose File New and choose a template in the Use Template list, and then choose OK.
3. Choose Tools Create Envelope, type an address in the Addressed To box, and choose Add to Document.
4. Click the envelope address frame to select it and then move the mouse onto the edge of the frame, away from the resizing handles, until the mouse cursor becomes a four-headed arrow. Drag the address frame to a new location.
5. To check your results, choose File Print Preview, or print the envelope.

To save the new address position as the default, follow these steps:

1. Move the insertion point into the envelope address.
2. In the Style box on the ribbon, choose envelope address (even though it already appears at the top of the style list), then click in the address.
3. Choose Yes at the prompt to redefine the style.
4. Choose Format Style.
5. In the Style Name box, choose envelope address, then choose Define.
6. Select the Add to Template check box and choose Change Close.
7. Choose File Save All and choose Yes at the prompt to save changes. Choose Yes again at the prompt to save global glossary and command changes.

Create envelope address files

If you frequently print envelopes addressed to the same individuals, create an *envelope file* for each. Follow these steps:

1. Open a new document and choose Tools Create Envelope.
2. Type the person's address and an optional return address, then choose Add to Document.
3. Save the file under an appropriate name—for example, SMITH.ENV.
4. To print an envelope, open the envelope file and choose File Print.
5. Type **0** in the From and To boxes, and choose OK.

Specifying a range from page 0 to page 0 tells Word to print only an envelope.

Use bookmarks to simplify envelope printing

If, while typing a document, you know that you will be printing one or more envelopes, you can mark the addressee and return address with special bookmarks that tell Word to insert their text in the Create Envelope dialog box. Follow these steps:

1. Select the return address and choose Insert Bookmark.
2. Type **EnvelopeReturn** in the Bookmark Name box and choose OK.
3. Repeat these steps for the addressee, but type **EnvelopeAddress** in the Bookmark Name box.

When you choose Tools Create Envelope, Word automatically displays the recipient's address and return address in the Create Envelope dialog box, so you don't have to retype them.

Save time printing multiple copies with downloaded fonts

When you print multiple copies of a document that uses downloaded fonts, you can save time if you start the print job in a nonstandard manner. If you simply choose File Print and set the number of pages to print, Word downloads the fonts before printing each copy of the file. To download the fonts just once for the entire print job, follow these steps:

1. Choose File Print.
2. Choose Setup twice, choose the number of copies you want to print, and then choose OK three times. After printing, you need to reset the number of copies to 1.

Use PostScript soft fonts for faster printing

Windows is set by default to download PostScript soft fonts each time you begin a print job. Your documents will print faster if you tell Windows to look for the fonts in the printer instead of downloading them for each document. You then can download the fonts just once from a batch file at the start of each printing session, as described later.

Open the WIN.INI file from the Windows subdirectory. You can edit WIN.INI in Word only if you remember to save it as a DOS text file.

If you have installed soft fonts, WIN.INI will have a section titled [PostScript, LPT1]. You need to find this section. (The LPT1 specification may be different if you're using a different printer port.)

Each soft font statement uses this format:

```
softfont1=c:\psfonts\pfm\cfr____.pfm,c:\psfonts\cfr____.pfb
```

To prevent Windows from downloading soft fonts each time you print a document, remove the `.pfb` portion of each soft font statement. After removing the `.pfb` section, the preceding sample statement should look like the following:

```
softfont1=c:\psfonts\pfm\cfr____.pfm
```

Before printing, download fonts to your printer by using the program supplied by the publisher of your soft fonts. If you're using Adobe Systems soft fonts, for example, use PSDOWN.EXE to download fonts to a serial printer or PCSEND.EXE to download fonts to a parallel printer.

Print text and graphics with the HP LaserJet II

If Word doesn't print pages that contain text and graphics on the LaserJet II, change the printer's FORM LENGTH setting. To change the FORM LENGTH setting, follow these steps:

1. Press the ON LINE button, and then press MENU until you see `FORM=` in the LCD window.
2. Press - (hyphen) until you see `FORM=60` and press Enter.
3. Press MENU until you see `00 READY` in the display window.
4. Hold down CONTINUE/RESET until you see `07 RESET`.

Avoid `Out of memory` **errors with PostScript printers**

If you're using a PostScript printer and create documents that contain text in portrait and landscape mode, you may receive an `Out of memory` message when you try to save your work. To work around this program bug, choose File Print Setup, and choose the Hewlett-Packard LaserJet III. You will be able to save your work without further problems. When you're ready to print the document, use File Print Setup to switch back to the PostScript printer.

7

CHAPTER

Working with Styles

Styles are one of Word's most effective timesaving features. With a style, you can apply extensive formatting commands with a single keystroke. You can assign multiple styles to their own templates for use with specific types of documents. When you change a style (for example, by choosing a new font), Word automatically reformats all the text in a document that has been formatted with that style.

Import styles quickly

If you want to use a style from another document, you don't have to use the style merge feature. Instead, copy a paragraph from the other document that uses the formatting you want. Make sure that the style's name isn't duplicated in the document you're copying to, or Word will format the imported paragraph with that style.

You can copy as many as 50 paragraphs that use styles with unique names. (If you copy more than 50 paragraphs, Word merges all the external document's styles with the current document.)

You can assign a paragraph formatted with a frequently used style to a Glossary item, and then insert it as needed. Follow these steps:

1. Select text formatted with the style you want to insert with a glossary and choose Edit Glossary.
2. Type a name for the item in the Glossary Name box and choose Define.
3. To insert the glossary, type the glossary name in a document—separated from nearby text with a space—then press F3; or choose Edit Glossary, choose the glossary name in the Glossary Name list, and choose Insert.

   To insert the glossary text without its style formatting, choose Edit Glossary, highlight the glossary's name, and choose Insert as Plain Text.

Use the style area to select a paragraph

If you have turned on the style area so Word displays style names in the left margin, you can click a paragraph's style name to select the paragraph. To turn on the style area, follow these steps:

1. Choose View Normal.
2. Choose Tools Options and type **v** to display View options.
3. In the Style Area Width box, set a number greater than 0 and choose OK.

Word displays style names in the left margin.

You can resize the style area by using the mouse (to display long style names or to show more of the typing area). Move the mouse cursor onto the vertical line that separates the style area from text. When the mouse cursor becomes a double vertical line, press the mouse button and drag the style border left or right. To close the style area, drag the vertical divider to the left and off the screen.

Switch from individual formatting commands to styles

If you format paragraphs with individual commands from the Format menu and then decide that you want to format the paragraphs with styles, select the paragraphs and press Ctrl+Q. Word removes all individual formatting and returns all formatting to the styles assigned to the paragraphs. (If no style is selected, Word applies the Normal style.) This capability is especially useful for desktop publishing when you may want to experiment with individual formatting commands and decide to use an existing style, instead.

Think twice before changing NORMAL.STY

Remember that Word uses the Normal style as the basis for all the standard styles supplied with the program. Changing the Normal style changes all the related styles; therefore, don't change the Normal style unless you want to change the standard styles, as well. Instead, create new body text styles based on the Normal style for use in special situations.

Use a base style to change similar styles quickly

Tired of making minor changes to separate similar styles? Create a base style that contains all the features shared by the styles. You then can change all the styles by editing the base style. Keep an eye open for design elements that naturally fall in "families," such as headings, body text (which can serve as a base style for indented quotations, lists, two-column sidebars, and so on). To create a base style, follow these steps:

Before you begin, create a style (the base style) that includes formatting commands shared by the style family.

1. To base a second style on the first style, choose Format Style Define.
2. In the Style dialog box, type a name, description, and shortcut key, if any, and type the name of the base style in the Based On box.
3. Change any formatting options for the new style. Choose Change and choose Close or Apply.

To change the base formatting for all the family's styles, you only have to edit the base style.

Convert styles from Word for DOS

If you have switched from Word for DOS to Word for Windows, Word automatically converts your old style sheets when you load a Word for DOS document. If Word can't find the style sheet that was created for the old document, the program prompts you for the style sheet's path and file name. If you can't locate the style sheet, or if it no longer exists, Word imports the document as plain text.

Delete a style from a template

You sometimes may want to remove styles from templates—for example, if you no longer use the style and don't want it to appear in the style lists. To delete a style from a template, follow these steps:

1. Choose File Open and in the List Files of Type list box, type ***.dot** to choose Document Templates. Then choose the template in the File Name box and choose OK.
2. Choose Format Style and in the Style Name box, choose the style you want to delete. Then choose Define.
3. Choose Delete and enter Yes at the prompt to delete the style, and then choose Close.
4. Choose File Save, and then choose File Close.

Create styles for section formatting

You can't save section formatting in a Word style, but you can save section marks in glossaries. Follow these steps:

1. Format the section whose formatting you want to save. Choose Insert Break, choose the type of section break you want to insert, and then choose OK.
2. Choose View Normal. Move the cursor onto the section mark (a double dotted line).
3. Choose Format Section Layout, make formatting selections, and choose OK.
4. Select the section mark and choose Edit Glossary. Type a glossary name and choose Define. When you exit Windows, enter Yes at the prompt to save global changes.

Use Replace to format text with a different style

You can use Replace to reformat text from one style to another. Follow these steps:

1. Choose Edit Replace Styles.

2. In the Find What Style list box, choose a style, and then choose OK. Notice that Word displays the name of the style at the `Format:` prompt below the Find What text box (unless no style was selected).

3. Move the insertion point to the Replace With box and choose Styles. Choose a style for the replacement, then choose OK. Notice that Word displays the name of the replacement style at the `Format:` prompt below the Replace With text box.

4. Choose Match Case, then choose Replace All.

CHAPTER 8

Working with Fonts

Word uses the Microsoft Windows graphical environment to display fonts on-screen approximately as they will appear when printed and how they will affect line breaks on the printed page. You can choose fonts with the ribbon or with menu commands. You also can assign repeated font choices to styles. The tips in this chapter will help you work more effectively with the fonts supported by your printer.

Activate TrueType fonts

If you install TrueType fonts but they don't appear in Word's font lists, perform the following steps to ensure that you're using the correct Windows 3.1 or later driver:

1. Choose File Print Setup. Select the printer you have installed, then choose Setup.

2. If Word displays an About or Info button, choose it and verify that the driver you're using is designated as a Windows 3.1 driver. Choose OK until you return to the document screen.

3. To check if the TrueType fonts are now available, choose the Font menu on the ribbon or choose Format Character.

If TrueType fonts still are not available, make sure that TrueType fonts are enabled under Windows. From the Program Manager, open the Main group and choose Control Panel Fonts TrueType. Make sure that the Enable TrueType Fonts check box is marked. Choose OK. Choose Close and close the Control Panel and Main group.

Use Ctrl+F to change fonts quickly

To switch to another font quickly, press Ctrl+F, type the font name in the font list box on the ribbon, and press Enter.

To change the point size quickly, press Ctrl+P, type the new font size in the point size list box on the ribbon, and press Enter.

Superscript and subscript text quickly

To superscript text by three points quickly, select the text and press Shift+Ctrl+=. To subscript text by three points, select the text and press Ctrl+=.

Adjust spacing after large fonts

Heading text in a large, boldfaced font looks ugly if you let Word insert normal line spacing for the large font between the heading and the body text that follows. To close up the spacing between headings and text, change the paragraph formatting for the heading style. With the insertion point in a heading, choose Format Style Define Paragraph and set a small space (for example, `0.5 li`, or a small measurement expressed in inches) in the After box. Then choose OK to return to the Style dialog box.

Use Ctrl+F2 to scale fonts quickly

To quickly increase or decrease the point size of a font, select the text and press Ctrl+F2 or Ctrl+Shift+F2. In Page Layout View, you will see the font "grow" and "shrink" on-screen. You also can read the new size in the font size box in the ribbon.

With scalable fonts, Word changes the size in one-point increments. If the current size is 20.5 points, for example, the next bigger size is 21.5 points. If the font isn't scalable, Word chooses the next available size.

Use unavailable fonts

You can format Word documents with fonts that aren't available on your printer. This capability is useful, for example, if you're sending a document to a commercial printer for typesetting or if you're formatting text for other users. Just type the font name in the font box in the ribbon. Word chooses the screen font that is closest in appearance to the chosen font.

Install new fonts on the ribbon

If newly installed fonts don't appear in the font list on the Word ribbon, choose File Print Setup Setup and choose OK twice. Word updates the ribbon to include the new fonts.

Change Word's default font

To change the default font, follow these steps:

1. Choose File Open, type **normal.dot** in the File Name box, and choose OK.

2. Choose Format Style Define Character.

3. Choose a font from the **F**ont list box and a point size in the **P**oints box. Choose OK. Choose Apply and choose **Y**es when Word asks if you want to change the properties of the standard style.

The font you choose immediately becomes the new default. When you exit Word, choose **Y**es when Word asks if you want to save the global glossary and command changes.

9

CHAPTER

Working with Templates

Templates are like roadmaps for documents. You can create templates that contain text, styles, automatically running macros, customized menus, and special toolbar buttons. When you need to create a special document type such as a desktop-published report, just open a new document and select the report template. You then can format the document by using styles and other commands specially created for that type of document.

To apply a template, choose **F**ile **N**ew, select the appropriate template from the template list, and choose OK. After selecting a template, you can choose template-specific styles, macros, and glossaries by selecting them from the appropriate program menus. You also can customize Word's program menus, adding menu choices with template-specific items that run macros (a menu choice named Print Statements, for example).

To create a template, follow these steps:

1. Choose **File New**, choose **Template** in the New box, and choose OK.

   You now can create text, styles, macros, or glossary entries for the template. (Be sure to choose the Template option in dialog boxes that you use to create styles, macros, or glossary items.)

2. To save the template, choose **File Save**, type a template name, choose OK, fill in any desired summary information, and choose OK again.

Word automatically gives the template name a DOT file name extension.

For a demonstration of what you can do with Word templates, try some of the sample templates supplied with the program. For example, choose **File New**, choose MEMO2 in the Use Template list, and click OK.

Create a letterhead template

A letterhead template is one of the most useful documents you can create with Word. When you open the template, Word displays your letterhead, ready to be filled in and laser-printed. You even can have Word fill in the current date and move the cursor to the first line of the address area.

To begin creating a letterhead template, follow these steps:

1. Choose **File New**, choose **Template** in the New box, choose NORMAL, and then choose OK.

2. Format your letterhead using decorative fonts, lines, frames, and imported graphics.

3. Where you want the date inserted, choose **Insert Bookmark**, type **Date** in the Bookmark Name box, and choose OK.

You will not be able to see the bookmark in the editing window, but Word will know it's there.

You can automate your letterhead with an AutoNew macro that runs automatically when you load the template. Follow these steps:

1. Choose **Tools Record Macro**. In the Record Macro Name box, type **AutoNew**, then choose OK.
2. In the document window, choose **Edit Go To**, type **Date**, and choose OK. To have Word insert the current date, choose **Insert Field**.
3. Choose the Create date field in the Insert Field Type list. In the **Instructions** list, choose a date format, then choose **Add** and OK.
4. Move the cursor to the first address line, and then choose **Tools Stop Recorder**.
5. Delete the date so Word doesn't use the template creation date when the automatic macro runs. Save the file under a descriptive name such as LHEAD.
6. To write a letter, open a new file and choose the LHEAD template. Word loads the template and runs the macro that inserts the date and places the cursor at the first address line.

Start Word with your own choice of template

The default template that Word applies when you open a new document is NORMAL.DOT. When you open a new file by choosing **File New**, you can select a different template in the New dialog box. If you frequently use a template other than NORMAL.DOT, you can set Word to display that template's name as the default in the New dialog box.

Follow these steps to change the default template:

1. Press Alt+Esc to switch to Program Manager. Choose the Word icon and choose File Properties.

2. In the Command Line box, add the /n switch so the command line looks like the following (the path will be different if you have installed Word in another subdirectory):

   ```
   C:\WINWORD\winword.exe /n
   ```

   After adding the /n parameter, Word starts without opening a new document.

3. Choose OK and press Alt+Esc to switch back to Word. Choose Tools Macro, and in the Macro Name box, type **autoexec**. Then choose Edit.

4. In the macro editor, type the following macro, where *template name* is the name of the template you want to use as the new default. Be sure to type the name of the template in quotation marks.

   Sub MAIN
   FileNew .NewTemplate = 0, .Template = "*template name*"
   End Sub

5. Choose File Close and choose Yes at the prompt to save changes. When you exit Word, choose Yes at the prompt to save global changes.

When you load Word, it opens a new document based on the template named in the macro. Opening a new file by choosing File New, however, displays the New dialog box with the default NORMAL template selected.

Use template reminders

When creating a new template, it's essential that you understand the formatting of the template when you later retrieve and use it. To refresh your memory, type a few words of descriptive text in each new section of the template—for example, **Type the address here**, **Two-column format for Bits & Pieces column begins here**, and so on.

Convert templates to documents

If the Save As dialog box displays only template files (files with a DOT extension), and most of the options in the Save As dialog box are grayed, this signifies that the on-screen file has been saved as a template and not as a document. Before you can use the Save As dialog box to export the file to another word processor format, you need to convert the file to a document. To do so, follow these steps:

1. Display the template on-screen and choose **E**dit Select **A**ll or press Ctrl and keypad 5 to select the whole document. Choose **E**dit **C**opy (Ctrl+C).
2. Open a new document window. Choose **F**ile **N**ew, and OK.
3. Choose **E**dit **P**aste (Ctrl+V) to insert the contents of the other window from the Clipboard.
4. To save the file as a document, choose **F**ile Save **A**s, choose a file format and type a document name, and then choose OK. If Word is set to display the Summary Info dialog box, choose OK again.

Save customized templates

Toolbar buttons, keyboard shortcuts, macros, and menu items you customize can be saved with specific templates or for global use with all templates.

You, for example, may want to save keyboard shorcuts in a special template for working with documents that contain lots of tables. You also may want to design a template that includes a toolbar button for inserting annotations when you work with drafts shared with co-workers.

To save customized shortcut keys, toolbars, macros, and menus, you must first attach them to an existing template. Follow these steps:

1. Choose File Template and in the Attach Document To list, choose a template. Don't choose the NORMAL template because that template makes the customized options available for all documents.
2. Type an optional template description in the Description box, and then choose OK.
3. To attach your changes to a new template, before you begin customizing, choose File New Template, accept the default NORMAL template, and choose OK.
4. Make your customization changes, choose File Save, type a new template name, and choose OK.

10

CHAPTER

Working with Frames

Frames are one of Word's most important desktop publishing tools. You can place pictures, WordArt objects, charts, tables, and spreadsheet data in frames. You can resize frames and tell Word to keep a frame in the same position on the page when adjacent text changes, or you can have Word move the frame together with the surrounding text.

Create a frame that expands when you add text

Word's text frames don't automatically expand if you try to add more text than they can hold—you must enlarge the frames manually. To place text in a box that automatically expands, create a single-cell table with borders. Follow these steps:

1. Choose Table Insert Table. In the Insert Table dialog box, type **1** in the Number of Columns box.
2. In the Column Width box, choose Auto or enter a fixed column width, then choose OK.
3. With the cursor in the table cell, choose Format Border. Choose Box or Shadow.

4. In the Line box, choose a line format for the borders.
5. In the Border box, choose any borders you want to omit. For example, if you choose all the borders but one, only the unselected border is applied.

   Pull-quotes are often formatted with only top and bottom borders. (A *pull-quote* is a passage pulled from the main text and placed in a separate box, formatted in a larger font. The purpose of pull-quotes is to draw the reader's attention to an important point in the text.)
6. If you want the text shaded, choose Shading and choose a custom shading pattern and background.

   If you print the document on a laser printer, shading darker than 5% may decrease the readability of text. If you export the document for printing on a typesetting machine, 10% shading should be readable.
7. Choose OK until you return to the document window.

The table cell expands and contracts to accommodate editing changes. You can format the text with styles or apply individual formatting commands (for example, to align a pull-quote with right justification).

Place a frame around a table row

If you place a frame around a table row, Word may reformat the table according to its rules for wrapping text in a frame, changing the size of the table row. To avoid this problem, turn off wordwrap for the frame. To place a frame around a table row, insert the frame around the row. Select the frame and choose Format Frame. In the Text Wrapping box, choose None and then OK.

Remove frame borders

When you create a frame and then choose Format Frame Remove Frame, Word doesn't delete the frame borders. To remove the borders, position the cursor inside the borders and press Ctrl+Q. This action removes the frame borders; it also removes paragraph formatting from text in the frame, so you may need to reformat the paragraph.

Another way to remove the unwanted borders is to position the cursor inside the borders and choose Format Border None and OK. This process also removes formatting from text in the frame.

Resize frames easily

Resizing an empty frame is much quicker than resizing a frame that contains a graphic image. If you work with an empty frame first, it's also less likely that you will need to resize the frame later.

If you import an image and then place it in a frame, Word resizes the frame to fit the image. When you create a frame first then import an image, however, Word sizes the image to fit in the frame.

The same rules apply to placing charts in frames. Keep this fact in mind when you place charts and graphics on complex pages where oversized images may ruin your page design.

Avoid problems mixing styles and frames

Applying a style to text that contains a frame deletes the frame, unless the style definition contains a frame. Applying any of the standard heading styles, for example, deletes a frame created with the Normal style.

To work around this problem when creating frames, apply styles first, then create the frames. If you accidentally delete a frame, choose Edit Undo (Ctrl+Z).

Preview frames before printing

If you use a laser printer, always check your work with Print Preview before printing the text. Frames placed too far into the margins are truncated if they fall within a laser printer's nonprinting page margins.

Create frames with double borders

You can create frames with double borders by using the double border styles offered in Word. You also can create some interesting effects with a little-known method for creating double borders. This technique provides an interesting way to place a graphic image inside a frame and place its caption in a second, larger frame. Follow these steps:

1. Create a frame, select the frame and choose Format Border, choose border options, and choose OK.

   To add a second border:

2. Click the paragraph mark at the right end of the ribbon to display the hidden paragraph mark next to the lower right corner of the frame (if it isn't already visible).

3. Click the paragraph mark to place the insertion point between the frame and the paragraph mark.

4. Choose Format Border, choose border settings, and choose OK. Word creates a second border around the frame.

   If you create a second border in single-column text, the second border extends all the way across the page. To make the second frame narrower:

5. Click the paragraph mark again and choose Format Paragraph.
6. Increase the From Right setting in the Indentation box and choose OK.

   To add a caption:

7. Press Enter to add space below the graphic image, then type the caption's text.

Format text that wraps around a frame

To tell Word to wrap text around a frame, follow these steps:

1. Create the frame, and then size and position it on the page.
2. Click the frame to select it, choose Format Frame, and choose Around in the Text Wrapping box.
3. To customize the distance between the frame and wrapped text, choose a new measurement in the Distance from Text box and choose OK.

CHAPTER 11

Working with Tables

Word's automatic table features are a benefit for users who must format text and numbers in columns and rows. You can import spreadsheet data into a table, and you can create your own tables that perform spreadsheet-type calculations. The following tips will help you use tables more effectively.

Create running table headers

To repeat column headings after a page break, perform the following steps:

1. Choose View Normal. Select the header you want to appear at the top of the page.
2. Choose Edit Copy.
3. Choose View Header/Footer. Choose Header and OK.
4. Choose Edit Paste Close. Select the original header.
5. Choose Table Delete Rows.

To view the results of your work, choose File Print Preview.

Keep table column headings visible on-screen

Working in a table or merge data entry screen can be frustrating when you add a sufficient number of rows to make the header row scroll off the top of the screen. To keep the header row in view, split the window and open a second copy of the document in the second window. Choose Window New Window and drag the split box down from the top of the vertical scroll bar. Open a copy of the document in the second window. Your changes are reflected in both copies of the document, but only the document in the active window scrolls while you work.

Make tables that move

To create a table you can position anywhere on the page by dragging it with the mouse, put the table in a frame. Follow these steps:

1. Choose Table Insert Table, select the number of rows and columns for the table, and choose OK. (Or use the Table button in the Toolbar to create a table.)
2. With the insertion point anywhere in the table, press Alt+5 on the numeric keypad, or choose Table Select Table to select the table.
3. Choose Insert Frame. If you aren't currently in Page Layout view, Word asks if you want to switch to Page Layout view now. Choose Yes.

   Word places the table in a frame.

To format the frame with borders and shading:

1. Click the frame to select it, then optionally choose Format Border.
2. Choose border and shading options, then choose OK.

To move the table with the mouse:

1. Click outside the frame, then move the mouse cursor into the frame.
2. When the cursor turns into a four-pointed arrow, drag the frame to a new location.

To resize the frame and table with the mouse, click the frame and drag a sizing handle.

Use a shortcut for moving table rows

To move a table row up or down quickly, select the entire row, then press Shift+Alt+up arrow or down arrow. You don't have to be in Outline mode for this action to work.

Add table columns quickly

To add table columns to the right of existing columns, select from the table as many columns as you want to add. To select columns, drag across the columns with the right mouse button. Then choose Edit Copy (Ctrl+C). Move the insertion point to the right end of the first row of the table and choose Edit Paste (Ctrl+V). Any text in the column is copied along with the column cells. To delete the text, select the column by pressing the right mouse button anywhere in the column, then press Del.

Delete tables or table rows

To delete a table:

1. Select the table. Press Alt, A, A (hot keys for choosing Table Select Table) or press Alt+5 on the numeric keypad.
2. Choose Table Convert Table to Text, choose a separator option, and choose OK. To delete the text, press Del.

   or

Choose Table Delete Rows. (This action deletes the table along with its text.)

or

Select the table (or a section of the table) and at least one paragraph marker below the table, then press Del.

Adjust table column widths

After formatting a table, you may find that you need to re-align table columns. Follow these steps:

1. Move the cursor into the cell whose borders you want to align, then choose Table Select Column.
2. In the ruler, click the symbol at the left end until it turns into a left bracket ([).
3. Drag the *T-markers* in the ruler to adjust the column width.

To adjust multiple column widths more precisely, use the keyboard. Follow these steps:

1. Select the table. Press Alt, A, A (hot keys for choosing Table Select Table) or Alt+5 on the numeric keypad.

   To adjust selected columns with the keyboard, use Shift and the arrow keys to select columns. To adjust a single column width, place the insertion point in the desired column and follow step 2.

2. Choose Table Column Width, type a dimension in the Width of Columns box, and choose OK.

Change table column widths in three ways

You can change the width of an individual table cell or a group of cells without affecting the width of the table in three ways. Following is the first:

1. Select the cell or group of cells.

   Be sure to select the gridline to the right of the cell or group of cells. With the gridline selected, the mouse pointer becomes a double arrow (see fig. 11.1).

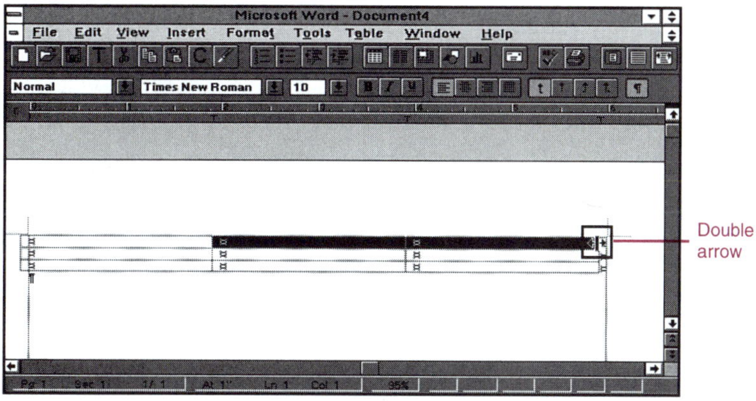

Fig. 11.1 *Table cells selected with the mouse cursor displayed as a double arrow.*

2. Hold down Shift and drag the gridline to a new position.

In the second method for changing column widths, you adjust column widths individually.

Word doesn't let you adjust text column widths individually with the ruler or with the Format Columns command. The User's Guide recommends placing unequally-sized columns in a table and adjusting the cell widths. A problem arises, however, with dividing the text: If you select the text and choose Table Convert Text to Table, Word asks if you want to divide the text into cells at paragraph marks, tabs, or commas—none of which is appropriate.

Instead, insert an empty table in the text. Follow these steps:

1. Choose Table Insert Table, specify two columns and one row, and choose OK. Or create a table with the Table button in the Toolbar.
2. Cut and paste the text into the table and use cut and paste again to divide the text equally between cells.

To adjust the space between columns (the *gutter*):

1. Move the insertion point anywhere in the table and choose Table Column Width.
2. Choose a measurement in the Space between Cols box and choose OK. (For two-column text, .3" looks fine; .5" is too wide.)

Following is the third way to adjust column widths. This time, you use the ruler.

To perform precise adjustments on table column widths quickly, click the left end of the ruler until the left bracket symbol ([) appears, then double-click the T-shaped column marker you want to adjust. Word displays the Column Width dialog box where you can specify column width and space between columns in hundredths of an inch. To set the width of other columns without leaving the dialog box, click the Previous Column or Next Column button.

Split a table

What do you do if you're creating a table and decide you want to split the table and insert a paragraph of text between the sections? Move the cursor to where you want to split the table and press Ctrl+Shift+Enter. Word splits the table, and you now can type new text in the space between the halves.

Select a table

To select an entire table, you can move the cursor into the first cell of the first row, then press F8 to enter extended selection mode, and press Ctrl+End to extend the selection to the end of the table. To turn off the selection and leave extended selection mode, press Esc. You also can select a table by pressing Alt+keypad 5 or Alt, A, A (the hot keys for choosing Table Select Table).

Select a table row by using a macro

If you do a lot of work using tables, you may find it useful to create a macro that selects the row that holds the cursor. Follow these steps to create the macro:

1. Choose Tools Macro, and type a macro name—for example, **SelectRow**—then choose Edit.
2. In the macro editor, type the macro as shown:

   Sub MAIN
   StartOfRow
   EndOfRow 1
   End Sub

3. Choose File Close, and choose Yes at the prompt to save your changes.
4. To run the macro, choose Tools Macro, select the macro, and choose Run.

You can assign the macro to a shortcut key or a Toolbar button, by choosing Tools Options Keyboard or Toolbar, and choosing shortcut key or button options in the dialog box.

Align table rows

Aligning table rows left, right, and center on the page has nothing to do with row height—or so you may think! To align rows select the row(s), choose Table Row Height, click the Left, Center, or Right button, and choose OK.

This trick is useful for formatting text in parallel columns with a table. For example, you can specify right-alignment for the text in the left column and left-alignment for the text in the right column. This may be useful if, for example, you create a program for a music concert and list the players in the left (right-aligned) column and their instruments in the right (left-aligned) column.

You then can adjust cell and column widths to lay out the table text in two lines per cell to fit more text in each line so the table fits on the page. This procedure may displace table borders and destroy the alignment of text. To realign the table text, select the entire table (press Alt+5) and choose Table Row Height Left and OK.

Create tables with styles

If you spend a lot of time formatting tables with borders, shading, text alignment, and so on, you can save time by assigning the table formatting commands to a style. You then can apply the style to other tables with a single command. This procedure is a good way to ensure consistent formatting for all tables (see fig. 11.2).

Store tables as glossaries

If you frequently use the same table format, you can store the format as a glossary and retrieve it with a few keystrokes. Table glossaries are very useful for phone message or memo forms and other situations where you may want to insert a preformatted form quickly. To store a table as a glossary, select the first row of the table. Choose Edit Glossary, type a glossary name, and choose Define.

When you want to insert a table, type a space and the glossary name, and press F3. Word deletes the name and inserts the table. You also can choose Edit Glossary, choose the table glossary, and choose Insert.

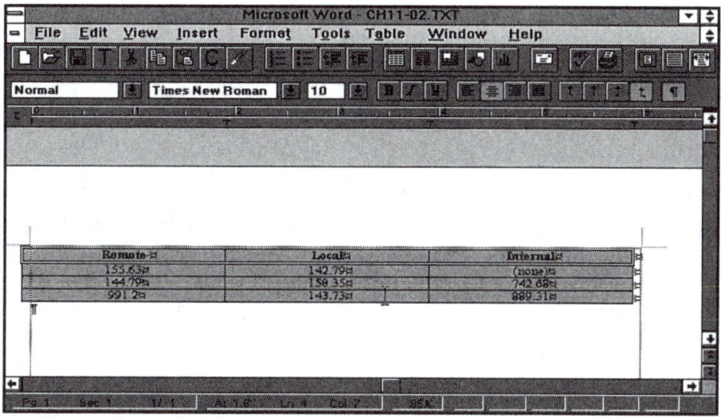

Fig. 11.2 *A formatted table.*

If the table saved as a glossary item isn't long enough, you can insert a new row at the end of the table. Move the cursor into the rightmost cell of the last row and press Tab.

Format paragraphs in tables

When you create a table, remember that the paragraph formatting for text in the table is the same as the formatting of the paragraph above the table. Text, therefore, may not align the way you expected because text paragraph indentation is added to the default distance between cell borders and text.

To fix this problem, set paragraph indents for text in the table by following these steps:

1. With the cursor in the table, press Alt+5 on the numeric keypad to select the table.

2. Choose Format Paragraph, set all indentations to 0, and choose OK.

Create borders around table text

When you add a border around the text in a table cell (with the Format Border command), Word formats the table cell borders. You may not want to do this—for example, when you want the text to have its own borders, separate from the cell borders. To place borders around the text only, follow these steps:

1. Select the paragraph marker at the end of the text for which you want to create a border. To insert a paragraph mark, press Enter at the end of the text. When you add a border in step 2, Word removes the extra line following the paragraph mark.

2. Choose Format Border, choose Box or Shadow, choose options for line style, color, and shading, and choose OK.

Use math in a table

You can perform simple spreadsheet-like calculations in tables. Follow these steps:

1. Choose Table Insert Table, specify the number of columns and rows, and choose OK. You also can use the table button on the Toolbar to create a table.

2. Position the cursor in a cell where you want to display the results of a calculation. Choose Insert Field.

3. In the Insert Field Type list, highlight = expression if it isn't already highlighted. Choose an optional number format in the Instructions list.

4. In the Field Code box, type the formula for the calculation. For a list of math expressions you can use and

rules for formatting expressions, move the cursor to = expression in the **Insert Field Type** list and press F1.

Word assumes row and column numbers from left to right and top to bottom. For example:

```
=sum ([r1c1:r4c1])
```

calculates the total of cells row 1, column 1 through row 4, column 1.

5. Choose OK.
6. If Word displays a `syntax error` message, choose **View Field Codes** to turn on field codes and correct your mistake.
7. To calculate the results of field codes in a table, press Alt+5 on the numeric keypad to select the table, and press F9 (Update Fields).

CHAPTER 12

Working with Print Merge

Word's Print Merge feature can insert variable text in each copy of a printed letter, such as names, addresses, and boilerplate text. Print Merge became much easier to use with Word 2.0, thanks to a new, step-by-step guided Print Merge setup procedure. This chapter presents tips for using Print Merge innovatively and more efficiently.

Print envelopes in reverse order for easy stuffing

Stuffing envelopes with print-merged letters is faster with the envelopes stacked upside down. To print-merge the envelopes in reverse order, follow these steps:

1. Print-merge the letters in normal order.

   Adjust the sort criteria to print envelopes or labels in reverse order by following these steps:

2. Open the data table and the merge document. Choose Tools Database Management Tools.

3. Choose Sorting. Choose a sort key in the Sort Key 1 list, and choose the Descending button, then choose OK.

4. Print-merge the envelopes as you normally would. Word prints the envelopes in descending order, as specified in step 3.

Sort comma-delimited data

Word can sort comma-delimited mail-merge data files exported from other programs such as WordPerfect, dBASE, and so on. Follow these steps:

1. Select the data file and choose Tools Sorting.

2. Choose Comma in the Separator box, and type or choose a number in the Field Number box (fields are numbered from left to right).

   Note: If the comma-delimited fields are enclosed in quotes, Word can't sort them correctly. You must first use Edit Replace to remove the quotes. In the Replace dialog box, type " in the Find What box and leave the Replace With box empty, then choose Replace All.

3. Select other sort options and choose OK.

Proofread comma-delimited data files

A helpful hint: Typing and proofreading comma-delimited data files in a small font is hard on the eyes. If you apply a very large font to the data file (36 points isn't too large), Word for Windows wordwraps the lines. You will find it easier, however, to sift through your data, and you still can apply a paragraph sort. (Remember to remove the large font before you use the file for a print-merge job!)

Proofread comma-delimited Print Merge data

You will find it easier to proofread comma-delimited data if you first convert the data to a Word table. Follow these steps:

1. Open the data file and press Ctrl+5 on the numeric keypad to select the entire file.
2. Choose Table Convert Text to Table.
3. Choose Commas and OK.

Formatting errors are immediately apparent—all the fields in one column may contain ZIP codes except for one record, for example.

If you need to convert the data back to comma-delimited format for use with another program, follow these steps:

1. Press Alt+5 on the numeric keypad to select the table, or choose Table Select Table.
2. Choose Table Convert Table to Text.
3. Choose Commas and OK.

You can use this method to convert comma-delimited data to a tab-delimited format. Convert the comma-delimited file to a table as described above, select the table, choose Table Convert Table to Text, and choose Tabs and OK.

Select inconsistent Mail Merge records

Standard Mail Merge record selection criteria such as ZIP code range, state, or income category may not be available for certain mail-merge jobs—for example, compiling a Christmas mailing list of personal friends.

A simple way to handle such cases is to create a new, appropriately named field (for example, Friends) and type **1** or another unique identifying key in the field for each record you want to include in selected mailings. You then can use the Record Selection dialog box to merge records with a 1 in the field. Follow these steps:

1. Choose File Open, type the main document's name, and choose OK.
2. Choose File Print Merge, and choose Attach Data File. Choose a data file and OK.
3. Choose Edit Data File.
4. With the insertion point anywhere in the datafile table, choose Tools Database Management Tools.
5. Choose Add New Field, type a name for the field (for example, **Friends**), and choose OK.

   Word adds a new field named Friends at the right end of the table.
6. Type **1** in the Friends field for each record that you want to use.
7. To select records before printing, open the main document and choose File Print Merge, and choose Merge.
8. In the Print Merge dialog box, choose Record Selection.
9. In the Record Selection dialog box, choose a field name (for example, Friends).
10. In the Is box, choose Equal to.
11. In the Compared To box, type a value that denotes records marked as Friends (for example, type **1**). Then choose Add Rule and OK.

12. Choose Merge to Printer or Merge to New Document, and choose OK.

Word merges and prints only the records for which the selection field (for example, Friends) is equal to the value you specified in step 10.

Set up a conditional merge

You can have Word insert different text in merge documents for different recipients, depending on test criteria in the data file. You may want to print one sentence for people whose billings total between $0 and $100, and another for people who owe over $100. All you need to do is insert an IF field in the merge document at the position where you want the data inserted:

```
{IF AmtDue >= $100 "{GLOSSARY OverC}" "{GLOSSARY UnderC}"}
```

In the preceding example, Word prints the text of the glossary entry `OverC` if the customer owes $100 or more, and the text of glossary entry `UnderC` if the customer owes less than $100.

If you have a lot of text to insert, replace the GLOSSARY fields in the example with INCLUDE fields, which enable you to insert the text of entire document files conditionally. For example:

```
{IF AmtDUE >= $100
  {INCLUDE C:\\WINWORD\\COLLECT1.DOC}
  {INCLUDE C:\\WINWORD\\COLLECT2.DOC}}
```

Notice that you must use double backslashes in an INCLUDE statement.

Control blank lines in a merge document

How can you avoid printing blank lines in a blank document when a field in a merge data file is blank—for example, if an address doesn't include a company name? Normally, Word deletes the blank line automatically. There are cases, however, where you may want to avoid printing a field's contents if it meets certain criteria. In such a case, you need to tell Word explicitly not to print a blank line.

Your data file, for example, may include a COMPANY field. In some records, the COMPANY field is blank and in others, the company name is U.S. Widget. In the latter case, you don't want to print the company name since it's the company you work for. Follow this example to format the address lines:

```
«FirstName»«LastName»
{IF «Company»«"{IF «Company» » "U.S. Widget"
"«Company»↓"}}«Street»
«City», «State»«Zip»
```

The nested IF statements work like this:

> IF the company name is not blank and IF it is not U.S. Widget, THEN print the company name and a newline character.

Notice that Word inserts a newline character only when it inserts a company name, thus avoiding blank lines.

Note: Don't use a paragraph mark instead of a newline character. Word may insert unwanted characters in the merged documents.

Type information from the keyboard during a merge

Word can pause and prompt you during a merge to enter special text from the keyboard. You may want to add, for example, a personal P.S. message at the end of a letter to your sales reps.

Insert a statement at the end of the merge document, formatted like the following example:

```
{Fillin "P.S. for «FirstName» «LastName»" \d "A
personal message from Jim Newcomb: "}
```

During a merge, Word pauses at the end of each letter and displays a dialog box with the message `"P.S. for` *recipient's name*`"`. The dialog box contains a text box where you can type your personalized message. Word inserts the text you specified following the optional \d switch in the Fillin statement: `A personal message from Jim Newcomb:`. (The \d switch tells Word to automatically insert the following text if you type nothing at the dialog box and press Enter.) You can delete the message or start typing after the colon. After typing a personal note, choose OK and Word merge-prints the next letter.

You also can tell Word to prompt you once for a personal note to be included at the end of each letter in a merge. Word displays the dialog box once. After you type a personal note and choose OK, Word automatically inserts the same note at the end of each letter. To perform this action, format the Fillin statement with an \o switch, like the following:

```
{Fillin "P.S. to «FirstName» «LastName» \o}
```

Include graphics in a print-merged document

You can include graphic images in print-merged documents, and you can tell Word to insert a different graphic into each merged document. One possible use of this technique is to include different graphic images for employees in various sales regions around the country.

To import different images during a merge, follow these steps:

1. Add a field to the data file that contains the file name of the image you want printed in each merged document.
2. In the main merge document, insert a field code where you want the graphic images printed:

```
{IMPORT "C:\\winword\\graphics\\{MERGEFIELD image}.bmp"}
```

Remember to include quotation marks around the file name and double backslashes in the path.

Word merges the image *file name* from the "image" field in the database. The IMPORT command then retrieves the graphic image.

Print-merge with dBASE data files

Word has the ability to print-merge data stored in the popular dBASE file format. Follow these steps to print-merge using dBASE data:

1. Choose File Print Merge.
2. Choose Attach Data File.
3. In the dialog box, choose the dBASE file, then choose OK. You don't have to attach a header file because Word can read header information from the dBASE file.
4. Create your main document as you normally would, using the Insert Merge Field button to insert merge fields.
5. To begin the merge, Choose File Print Merge Merge.

Mail Merge tips and traps

Despite the ease with which you can create and manage print-merge documents and data files with the menu-driven commands introduced in Word for Windows 2.0, merging and printing can still be tricky. The following tips will save you hours of looking for answers in the User's Guide.

In the data file:

- When you first set up your data file, be careful to create a separate column for each field you may later use to sort and select data for print-merging. If you plan to sort by ZIP code, for example, create a separate ZIP field column. It's much easier to type the ZIP codes separately than to go back later and delete and retype them in a separate field.
- Remember that in a data file formatted as a Word table, a field entry can be multiple lines or even paragraphs. You, therefore, can set up a field for freeform text entries.
- You can easily add a new, numbered field to a data file that you have set up as a Word table. Display the data file with **F**ile Print **M**erge Attach **D**ata File **E**dit Data file. Place the cursor in the table, and click the N button in the toolbar. Word adds the new field and automatically numbers the records. Including a numbered field in a data file can be very useful when you want to print-merge letters for part of the data file on one day, and print the rest the next day.
- Print Merge field results are formatted with chevrons (`«»`). The result of `{MERGEFIELD FirstName}`, for example, is `«FirstName»`. To edit a field, place the cursor in the field and press Shift+F9, or choose **V**iew **F**ield Codes.
- Word automatically avoids inserting a blank line when a field in the data file contains no information. You can force Word to *include* a blank line for

selected records by inserting a line break after the merge field in the merge document, instead of a paragraph mark. (To insert a line break, press Shift+Enter.) When you print-merge the document, Word includes a blank line.

In Print Merge dialog boxes:

- You can use Less Than and Greater Than to compare text and numbers. You can choose LastName is Less than N, for example, to print records where the last name begins with A through M.
- If you're using a header file, make sure to attach the header file first, before you begin a print-merge; otherwise, Word uses the first record of your data file as a header.

Mailing labels and envelopes:

- If you want Word to skip blank lines in a label merge, make sure that each line in the mailing label template ends with a paragraph mark—not a newline character.
- To print only an envelope included in a document, use the PRINT command and choose a page range from 0 (zero) to 0 (zero).
- When you choose Tools Create Envelope, Word usually can determine the To and From addresses. You, however, can indicate these addresses explicitly by selecting the To and From addresses and creating bookmarks called EnvelopeAddress and EnvelopeReturn. Word then uses the text of these bookmarks when you choose Create Envelope.

13

CHAPTER

Working with Fields

Word 2.0 provides 57 fields that perform specialized tasks when inserted in your documents. You can insert fields that print the author name, creation date of a document, and the current date. You can use a field to display nonprinting notes to yourself and others. Fields also play a major role in such important Word functions as Print Merge, indexing, cross-referencing, and building tables of contents. The tips in this chapter will help you get the most from Word's powerful fields.

Select fields with the mouse

To select a field with the mouse, you don't need to carefully drag the mouse to highlight the field including its enclosing curly braces. Instead, just double-click one of the field's curly braces ({}).

Get help with field codes

Field codes aren't documented in the User's Guide. To find out what each field does and how to use it, you can use on-line help; but following is a quicker way:

1. Choose Insert Field.
2. Highlight a field in the Insert Field Type list.
3. Press F1 to get context-sensitive help.

Word displays the Help screen for that field.

Display field codes and results simultaneously

To toggle between the display of field codes and their results, you can press Shift+F9 or choose View Field Codes. This action is fairly convenient, but when you're working with lots of field codes—for example, when you're designing a fill-in form—it may be more helpful to view field codes and their results at the same time in separate windows.

You then can write a simple macro that switches to the window that shows results, updates all field codes, then switches back to the window where you're working with field codes displayed.

Follow these steps:

1. In a Word document, choose File New and OK. Then choose Window Arrange All.

   Open a copy of the document in each window:
2. Choose File Open, choose the file, and choose OK.
3. Press Ctrl+F6 to move to the next window.
4. With the insertion point in the window where you will be working with field codes displayed, choose Tools Record Macro.
5. Type a macro name and description, choose an optional shortcut key, and choose OK.

6. Press Ctrl+F6 (Next Window).
7. Press Ctrl+5 on the numeric keypad (to select document).
8. Press F9 (Update Field).
9. Press left arrow or right arrow (to cancel selection), and press Ctrl+F6 (next document).
10. Choose Tools Stop Recorder to turn off macro recording.
11. To run the macro, type the shortcut key or choose Tools Macro, choose the macro by name, and choose Run.

Update date and time fields

Word can update date and time fields automatically when you print a document. To activate this option, choose File Print Options, check the Update Fields box, then choose OK. The Update Fields option remains in effect from one Word session to the next, until you deselect it.

Insert date and time with fields

To insert today's date and/or the current time in a document, choose Insert Date and Time, choose a format, and choose OK.

Using the {createdate}, {date}, and {printdate} fields, you also can have Word display various useful dates in your documents. (For detailed instructions on using Word fields, choose Insert Field, select the desired field in the Insert Field Type list box, and press F1.)

Following is what the {date} fields do:

Field Code	Action
createdate	Inserts the date the document was created
date	Inserts the date the field was last updated (to update the date, select the field and press F9)
printdate	Inserts the date the document was last printed (date taken from the Summary Info dialog box)

Change the Windows date format

Word uses as its default for date field codes the short date format defined in the Windows Control Panel (MM/DD/YY). To change this default, choose Insert Field, and in the Insert Field Type list box, choose Date. Choose a date format from the Instructions list box, and then choose OK.

Now open the WIN.INI file. Choose File Open, type **c:\windows\win.ini**, and choose OK.

1. Find the section of WIN.INI labeled [Microsoft Word 2.0].
2. At the end of the section, on its own line, type **DATEFORMAT=MMMM DD, YYYY**, or any other date format.
3. Choose File Save As.

   Note: You *must* save the WIN.INI file in DOS text format or it will no longer work, and you will not be able to load Windows! Follow these steps to edit WIN.INI:

4. Choose DOS Text (*.tx8) in the Save File as Type list.
5. Choose OK.

To activate the new default date format, you need to reload Windows.

Insert the previous month's date

You can insert the previous month's date in a Word document automatically, without changing the DOS system date. Use the following field codes where you want the date inserted:

```
{QUOTE {IF {DATE \@ M} = 1 12 {={DATE \@ M} - 1}}/1/92 \@ MMMM}
```

To type the field, press Ctrl+F9 to insert empty field braces. Type the first code (**QUOTE**), type a space, and press Ctrl+F9 to insert the second pair of braces. Continue typing the code, pressing Ctrl+F9 each time to insert field braces.

To update the field code, move the cursor into the code and press F9. To see the results, choose View Field Codes, which turns off the display of field codes. If the current month is December, the result is November.

Create table of contents entries quickly

Instead of using Insert Field to create table of contents entries, you can save time by using the Insert Field key (Ctrl+F9).

Move the cursor to the point where you want to create a table of contents entry and press Ctrl+F9. A pair of field characters appears. Type **tc "*text*"**, where ***text*** is the text you want to appear in the table of contents. (Remember to enclose the text in quotes.)

Use tables of contents to navigate documents quickly

If you create a table of contents early in the process of assembling a long document, you later can use the table of contents as an aid to navigating the text. If you put the table of contents at the end of the document, you can press Ctrl+End from wherever you're working. This action takes you to the end of the document where you can check the table of contents to identify the page number you want. Then press F5 (Go To) to move quickly to the desired page.

Fix problems with incomplete field text

If a field that is supposed to show text displays only the first word of the text you specified, you probably forgot to enclose the remaining text in quotation marks. To fix the problem, move the cursor onto the field and press Shift+F9 to display the field codes. Then insert quotation marks at the beginning and end of the text.

Move between fields

You can quickly find the next or previous field in a document. To move to the next field, press F11 (or Alt+F1 if you don't have an F11 key). To find the previous field, press Alt+Shift+F11 or Alt+Shift+F1.

These shortcuts can't find the {xe} (index entry), {tc} (table of contents entry), or {rd} (referenced document) fields. To locate these fields, first display hidden text. Choose **T**ools **O**ptions **V**iew, and select the H**i**dden Text check box. Return to your document and choose **E**dit **F**ind to locate the desired field code. Figure 13.1 shows hidden text in a letterhead document to indicate where the typist should begin entering text.

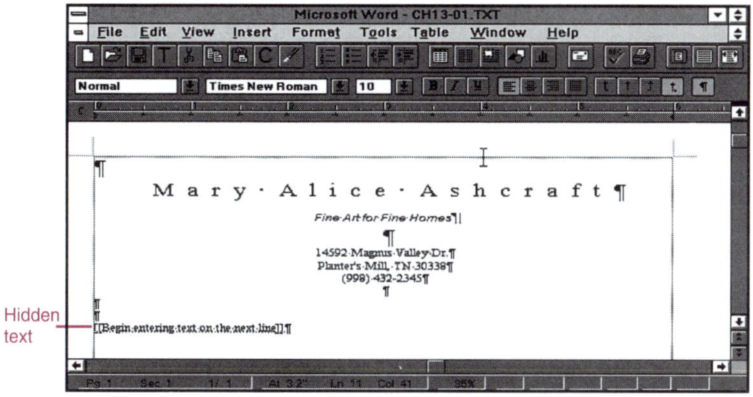

Fig. 13.1 *Hidden text.*

Type path names in fields

Certain fields such as {include}, {dde}, and {ddeauto} use DOS path names. When you type a path name in a field, you must use double backslashes (\\) wherever the path normally would have a single backslash.

You also must use a backslash before quotation marks that you want Word to display literally. To display the message

```
Type applicant's "QID" here:
```

in a fillin field, you need to format the field like this:

```
{fillin "Type applicant's \"QID\" here:"}
```

Create indexes using the XE field

Be careful when you type index entries using the XE (Index Entry) field. When you type an entry twice using different capitalization, Word creates separate index entries. For example, typing

{xe "Altruism: see Thoreau"}

creates the entry:

```
Altruism
see Thoreau,2
```

Whereas typing the following field:

{xe "altruism: see Thoreau"}

creates a separate entry:

```
altruism
see Thoreau,2
```

Create bookmarks easily

To insert a bookmark, you normally choose Insert Bookmark. To create bookmarks more quickly, follow these steps:

1. Position the cursor where you want to insert a bookmark, or select some text that you want to mark.
2. Press Ctrl+Shift+F5.

   No dialog box appears, but Word displays a prompt for a bookmark name in the status bar.
3. Type a name for the bookmark and press Enter.

Bookmarks aren't displayed, whether field codes are turned on or not.

Avoid losing bookmarks

If you create a bookmark and then move it to a new location with its surrounding text, you need to insert another bookmark at the original location if you want to have a bookmark there as well. Bookmarks are connected to the text where you originally insert them—not to the fixed location in the document where you insert them.

Name bookmarks carefully

When you create fill-in forms using the bookmark feature, be careful not to give any of the bookmarks one of Word's standard field names—for example, AUTHOR, DATE, or TIME. Word will automatically insert an author name, date, or time instead of allowing you to fill in data at the prompt.

Format bookmarks carefully

If you assign a bookmark to a number, be careful how you format the bookmark. To avoid mathematical errors in automatic calculations, be sure to include the space or tab on either side of the number when assigning it to a bookmark.

Prevent updating by locking individual fields

If you insert a date field in a document but don't want it updated each time you update the rest of the fields in the file, you can lock only that field. You may want to use invoices, for example, when you want the convenience of date fields but don't want the original invoice date to change. You also can lock fields other than the date field.

To lock a date field, follow these steps:

1. Select the field by double-clicking one of its curly braces, and then press Ctrl+F11 or Alt+Ctrl+F1 (Lock Field).
2. To unlock a field, select it and press Ctrl+Shift+F11 or Alt+Ctrl+Shift+F1.

Use fields in headers and footers

You can use Word fields to insert the current date and time and the file name of the on-screen document in headers and footers.

The steps that follow give instructions for creating a macro that inserts the date, time, and current file name in a header. To insert fields manually, omit steps 1 and 5 that start and turn off the macro recorder.

1. Choose Tools Record Macro, type a macro name and an optional shortcut key, and choose OK.

   Word displays REC in the status line to indicate that the macro recorder is active.

2. Choose Insert Field, press D and down arrow to choose Date, and choose OK.

3. Type a comma and a space, choose Insert Field, press T, down arrow twice to select Time, and choose OK.

4. Press Enter to place the file name on the next line, choose Insert Field, press F to select Filename, and choose OK.

5. Choose Tools Stop Recorder to turn off the macro recorder.

   To run the macro, press the macro's shortcut key or choose Tools Macro, choose the macro in the Macro Name list box, and choose Run.

6. To update the fields with the current date and time, or when you save the file under a new name, press Ctrl+5 on the numeric keypad to select the entire document, then press F9. If Word beeps and doesn't update the fields, this means that the fields are locked.

   To unlock all the fields in a document, choose Ctrl+5 on the numeric keypad, then press Ctrl+Shift+F11. To unlock an individual field, move the cursor into the field and press Ctrl+Shift+F11 or Alt+Ctrl+Shift+F1.

The purpose of locking fields is to prevent Word from updating them automatically when the document is printed or when you manually update all the fields in a document, as described earlier. To lock a field, choose View Field Codes, move the cursor onto the field, and press Ctrl+F11 or Alt+Ctrl+F1.

To have Word automatically update fields when you print a document, choose Tools Options, type P to choose Print options, select the Update Fields check box, and choose OK.

Use shortcut keys to work with fields

The following keys are useful for working with fields:

Key	Action
Ctrl+F9	Inserts the field characters {}
F9	Updates a field. (To update all the fields in a document, press Ctrl+keypad 5 to select the document, then press F9.)
F11	Jumps to the next field
Shift+F11	Jumps to the previous field
Shift+F9	Switches between field codes and results
Ctrl+F11	Locks field results to prevent updating
Ctrl+Shift+F11	Toggles between locking and unlocking a field. (To unlock all the fields in a document, press Ctrl+keypad 5 to select the document, then press Ctrl+Shift+F11.) Alternate key: Alt+Ctrl+Shift+F1
Ctrl+Shift+F9	Deletes a field code and permanently replaces the field with the text of its last result

Number items with the SEQ field

You can number anything in Word—photos, chapters, tables, figures, sketches, lists, references, and so on. A simple way to number is with the SEQ field. Follow these steps to number the tables in a document:

1. Place the cursor where you want to insert an automatic table number.
2. Type **table**, press the space bar, and choose Insert Field.
3. Select Sequence in the Insert Field Type list box.

   To obtain detailed information about the SEQ field, highlight Sequence and press F1 (Help).
4. Press Tab and type **table** after seq in the Field Code box.
5. Choose OK.

   Word inserts a field code: {seq table}.
6. Repeat the process for each table in the document. Word numbers the tables in sequence.

To create an SEQ field for a table quickly, press Ctrl+F9 to insert {} field characters and type **seq table** between the brackets. Before moving the cursor outside the brackets, press F9 to update the new field.

If you move a table and its SEQ field, you can update the fields to renumber all the tables in the document. Press Ctrl+5 on the numeric keypad to select the entire document, then press F9 (the Update Field key). To view the results, press Alt+Shift+F11 or Alt+Ctrl+Shift+F1 to turn off field codes.

Create cross-references with the SEQ field

You can use SEQ to create cross-references. Word then can update the cross-reference numbers automatically.

For clarity, the following steps use a specific example: a document that contains four tables, with an SEQ field assigned to each. With View Field Codes selected, the SEQ codes look like this:

```
Table {seq table}: Los Angeles Sales.
Table {seq table}: Chicago Sales.
Table {seq table}: Atlanta Sales.
Table {seq table}: Houston Sales.
```

With View Field Codes turned off and table references updated, the captions look like this:

```
Table 1: Los Angeles Sales.
Table 2: Chicago Sales.
Table 3: Atlanta Sales.
Table 4: Houston Sales.
```

You now decide to add a cross-reference to Table 4, Houston Sales. Follow these steps to create the cross-reference:

1. Select the {seq table} field code for Houston Sales.

   Select only the field code, not the rest of the caption or any spaces on either side of the field code.

2. With the Houston Sales SEQ field selected, choose Insert Bookmark, type a bookmark name (for example, **HoustonSales**), and choose OK.

   You can't use spaces in bookmark names, but you can use the underline character (_): **Houston_Sales**.

3. Move the insertion point to where you want to insert a cross-reference to the table. Place the insertion point, for example, after the word `Table` and the space in the following sentence:

   ```
   These figures are taken from Table .
   ```

4. Choose Insert Field and highlight Sequence.
5. In the Field Code box, type **table HoustonSales** after `seq` and choose OK.

Word inserts a field code in the following format:

```
These figures are taken from Table {seq table HoustonSales}.
```

Turn off the field codes display to see the result of your work:

```
These figures are taken from Table 4.
```

If you later move Table 4 in front of Table 3, you can update the reference. Press Ctrl+5 on the numeric keypad to select the document, then press F9 (Field Update key). Houston Sales becomes Table 3, and the cross-reference reads

```
These figures are taken from Table 3.
```

You can use the following "switches" to use the SEQ field codes in special ways:

Switch	Action
\c	Inserts the current or nearest preceding sequence number. *Example:* {seq table \c}
\n	Inserts the next sequence number. *Example:* {seq table \n}
\h	Hides the result of the field code. *Example:* {seq table \h}
\r*n*	Sets the sequence number to *n*. *Example:* {seq table \r15}

Create fill-in form fields that hold more than 255 characters

The Word for Windows User's Guide gives instructions for using the ASK and FILLIN fields, along with an AutoNew macro, to create fill-in forms for data entry. This method restricts the amount of data for each fill-in area to 255 characters. To work around this limitation, or if you prefer forms that don't use dialog boxes, follow this example:

1. Choose File New, choose the Template button, and choose OK.
2. Type data entry field labels, pressing Enter between entries. Press Ctrl+F9 to insert field code braces after each field label:

   Name: {}
   Address: {}

3. To see field code braces on-screen, choose View Field Codes.
4. To fill in the form, press F11 or Alt+F1 to jump to each pair of field braces, or press Shift+F11 or Alt+Shift+F11 to move to the previous field braces.

   When you press F11, the cursor moves to the next field.

5. Save the new template by choosing File Save As, type a name for the template, and choose OK.

You can use the empty field braces as bookmarks. The user then can jump to any fill-in field by name:

1. Choose View Field Codes to turn on the display of the field braces.
2. Select the first pair of braces, then choose Insert Bookmark.

3. In the Bookmark Name box, type the name of the field, then choose OK. Repeat the process for other fields.
4. To jump to a field, press F5 (Go To). Word displays a prompt in the status bar. Type the name of a field and press Enter.

14

CHAPTER

Desktop Publishing with Word for Windows

To be successful at desktop publishing, you must acquire a whole new set of skills. Not only must you know how to use Word for Windows formatting features, you also must know the art and science of document design. For centuries, typographers and graphic artists have compiled detailed rules for making text readable and documents pleasing to the eye. This chapter, therefore, deals with Word features and gives tips for laying out documents that invite rather than repel.

Systemize desktop publishing with templates

Establishing consistent formats for newsletters, catalogs, and other often-used documents involves endless tinkering. Instead of re-creating the steps each time you print a newsletter or catalog, for example, you can use the styles in a template. To create a template, follow these steps:

1. Open a new document: choose File New.
2. Choose the Template button and choose OK.
3. Choose File New and OK to open a second document window where you can experiment with formats for body text, headings and subheads, pull-quotes, drop caps, frames, captions, and so on.
4. When a section looks right, assign it to a style and copy the paragraph into the Document 1 screen. (To switch between windows, press Ctrl+F6.) Word copies the style along with the text.
5. Clear the Document 2 screen and work on the next design element. When the format is ready, repeat step 4.

When all the styles are completed, you have created a template for that document format. To save the template, choose File Save, type a name for the template, and choose OK. Choose OK at the Summary Info dialog box.

Concentrate on readability

The advent of laser printers introduced many new complexities to word processing, not the least of which was the question of how to use laser fonts for optimum readability.

Graphic designers distinguish between *legibility* (whether the eye can physically read type) and *readability* (whether type is pleasant and easy to read). To ensure that your documents deliver their message without annoying the reader, make sure that your documents use typefaces that are legible and readable.

Use sans serif type sparingly

People read sans serif type more slowly than serif type, and long passages set in sans serif typefaces are considered impersonal and dull. Exactly why this is so remains a subject for debate. As a general rule, use sans serif type only for pull-quotes, captions, and headlines. Figure 14.1 shows serif and sans serif typefaces.

Serif Typefaces:

This is Times Roman.

This is Bookman.

This is Zapf Calligraphic

Sans-Serif Typefaces:

This is Avant Garde.

This is Helvetica.

Fig. 14.1 *Examples of serif and sans serif typefaces.*

Use body text between 9 points and 12 points

The size of body text greatly affects a document's readability. The best size for body text is between 9 points and 12 points.

Note: Some fonts look larger than fonts of the same measured size because their *x-height* is larger. The x-height is the height of letters that don't have *ascenders* or *descenders*—for example: e, a, o, x, r (see fig. 14.2).

Fig. 14.2 *The elements of type.*

Compare fonts visually for readability

Some fonts look darker than others, and a font's *color* (darkness or lightness) may affect readability. To choose which of two fonts is more readable, set a few paragraphs in each and compare them side by side.

Use appropriate leading between lines of text

Line spacing, or *leading* (pronounced "ledding"), also affects readability. Text set with too little leading looks dense and unreadable; but too much leading also can inhibit readability. Studies show that one or two points of extra leading is best for body text set in normal column widths. For example, 10-point type set with 11-point leading in 20-pica lines is very readable.

The following table gives optimal leading and type size combinations for body text.

Type size (in points)	Minimum leading (in points)	Maximum leading (in points)
6	6	7
8	8	10
10	10	14
11	12	15
12	14	18
14	17	22

Choose line length based on font size

Very long lines of text inhibit readability, as do very short lines. The best line length is related to font size. Studies show that 10-point type is most readable when set in lines 18.9 picas long (about 3 1/6 inches). When 10-point text is set in 13.9 pica lines, readability falls by 10 percent. For 10-point text in 43.9 pica lines, readability drops another 11.4 percent.

A graphic designer's rule of thumb says that body type should be set in lines no longer than twice the width, in picas, of the current font size in points. For example, 10-point type should be set in lines no wider than 20 picas. But, as the following table shows, the rule of thumb breaks down for very small and very large text sizes.

Type size (in points)	Minimum length (in picas)	Maximum length (in picas)
6	8	10
8	9	13
10	13	16
11	13	18
12	14	21
14	18	24
18	24	30

Use ragged-right text for informal documents

Studies show little difference in the readability of justified and ragged-right body text, although slow readers find justified text harder to read. Sans serif fonts are slightly easier to read when set as ragged-right. In general, modern graphic arts practice leans toward using ragged-right margins for informal documents such as newsletters, flyers and brochures, and reports.

Overly ragged line endings slow down the reader. To avoid this problem, hyphenate ragged-right text. Many designers limit hyphenation to no more than two hyphenated lines in a row, and no more than three hyphenated words per paragraph.

Limit the use of italics, boldface, and underline

People read *italicized text* 20 words per minute slower than normal text. Limit the use of italics to photo captions, pull-quotes, foreign words, the titles of publications, and other brief text.

Boldface has no place in body text (with rare exceptions—for example, people's names in a company newsletter); neither does underlining, if you're using proportionally spaced laser fonts. The underline character was invented for typewriters that couldn't print italics. There is no underline character in formal typography.

Avoid setting words in CAPS

Type set in capital letters (caps) is hard to read. If you must set type in caps, use large and small caps.

Use only two typefaces per document

If you use more than one typeface in a document, limit your use to two typefaces only. Similar typefaces generally clash, while dissimilar ones may work well together—the classic examples are Times Roman and Helvetica, which coexist very well.

Create a page border

For flyers, brochures, and other desktop-published text, you may wish to create a line border around the page. Word doesn't include this capability as a standard option, but you can accomplish it with a simple workaround.

1. Choose Format Page Setup.
2. Choose the **Margins** button and type a minus sign before the measurement in the **Top** box, then choose OK.
3. Choose View Header/Footer Even Header and OK.
4. If the cursor isn't in a new paragraph, press Enter, and then move the cursor into the new paragraph.

5. Choose Format Border, and choose a preset border or specify a custom border, and then choose OK.
6. Choose Format Paragraph, and under Spacing in the At box, type **60li** (for 60 lines).
7. To have Word print the border outside the left and right margins, type a negative number in the From Left and From Right boxes. (For example, to print a border 1/4 inch outside the margins, type **-.25**.) Then choose OK.
8. If you're in Normal view, choose Close to close the header pane.
9. To view the results of your work, choose File Print Preview.

Format borders flush with margins

Borders that you place around paragraphs extend into the page margins. To align the borders flush with the margins, you must indent the paragraph by the width of the border. A double one-point lined border is three points in width, for example, so you need to indent the paragraph three points. Choose Format Paragraph, type **3 pt** in the left and right indentation boxes, and choose OK.

Use borders to create special effects

You can quickly insert text in a bordered box. The basic process follows:

1. Select the text you want to format with a border.
2. Choose Format Border. Choose border options for shading, lines, and a plain or shaded box, then choose OK.

You can use borders to create special effects. You can place text, for example, in a shadowed box with gray shading and lines only on the right and bottom sides. To edit border options, follow these steps:

1. Place the cursor in the bordered text and choose Format Border.

   In the Border Paragraphs dialog box, use the sample box in the Border box to view your changes.

2. To change the line style for one edge of the box, click that edge in the Border box, then choose a line style in the Line box.

To format a border edge without any lines, choose None in the Line box.

To change the shading of border lines, choose Color and choose Dk Gray or Lt Gray, or choose a color if your printer supports colors.

To change the shading of the background, choose Shading, choose a shade in the Background list, a pattern in the Pattern list (if desired), then choose OK.

Note: The Pattern list is important. For optimal readability, don't use background shading darker than 10% for typeset text and 5% for laser-printed text. Notice, however, that choosing Light Gray from the Color list in the Border Paragraphs dialog box prints a lighter shade of gray than choosing 5% in the Pattern list of the Shading dialog box.

You can create interesting effects by formatting boxes with shadowing and/or shading, with no lines or with lines only on selected edges.

Create special effects with headers and footers

You can create repeating text in a header or footer, then place the header or footer anywhere on the page. First, create the header or footer as you normally would, then turn on page layout view, select the header or footer, and choose Insert Frame. You then can drag the header or footer to the position where you want it to appear on each page.

You can make the frame invisible by formatting its borders. Choose Format Border, choose None in the Preset box, and choose OK.

You may want to print a *watermark* (very light text) under other page elements, for example, or place text or graphics in the left margin of each page. To print headers or footers in the text area, choose Format Page Setup, choose Margins, and insert a minus sign before the measurement in the Top or Bottom box.

Note: If you're not using a color printer, you can't create a watermark by specifying the Lt Gray font color in the Color list of the Character dialog box (opened by choosing Format Character). Font colors apply only to screen fonts, unless you're using a color printer or plotter.

Note: Word can't create shaded, shadowed, or outlined text, even with printers that support these features.

Print text in the left margin

To print text in the left margin (for headers, sidebars, running commentary, summaries, tips, and so on), the easiest method is to place the text in a frame. Choose Insert Frame and drag the crosshair cursor to draw the frame. If you start the frame in the wrong place, you can press Esc without releasing the mouse button to cancel frame drawing, or release the mouse button and move the frame. To move a frame, be sure you're in Page Layout view, then move the mouse cursor onto the frame border. The cursor turns into a four-pointed arrow. Now you can drag the frame to a new location. To type text into the frame, click in the frame and begin typing. Text wraps within the frame. To resize the frame, click the frame border to display the sizing handles and drag one of the handles. To give the frame borders, click the frame border and choose Format Border.

Create drop caps in Word for Windows 2.0

A *drop cap* is a large capital letter inset in the first lines of a paragraph. The procedure for creating drop caps in Word for Windows 1.1 was quite complicated, but a macro supplied with Word 2.0 makes it much easier. To install the drop cap macro, follow these steps:

1. Open the file named NEWMACRO.DOC, which Word installed in the WINWORD subdirectory.
2. In the dialog box that appears when you open the file, choose DropCap, and then choose Install.
3. In the second dialog box, choose a template into which you copy the macro. At this point, you also can choose a menu and/or shortcut key to assign to the macro.
4. Choose Cancel. Word copies the macro to the template you have selected.

To run the macro, position the cursor in a paragraph that you want to begin with a drop cap, then choose the macro from its menu or press its shortcut key. The macro turns the first letter in the paragraph into a drop cap.

Resize the frame or change the format to adjust a drop cap

Graphic designers are very fussy about the positioning of drop caps. The bottom of the drop cap, for example, must align flush with the baseline of the adjacent line of body text.

If Word doesn't place the drop cap perfectly, you can make minor adjustments by resizing its frame or by formatting the drop cap character as a superscript and adjusting its position in one-point increments. (A point is 1/72 of an inch.) To adjust the position of frame borders, click the frame and drag the frame handles. To adjust the position of the drop cap, select the drop cap letter and choose Format Character. Choose Superscript and apply an adjustment amount in points, and then choose OK.

Create your own drop caps in WordArt or Microsoft Draw

For a special effect, experiment with creating drop caps in WordArt or Microsoft Draw and placing them in frames for easy positioning.

Create typeset quotation marks

To insert inverted opening and closing single or double quotes, you can hold down Alt and type the appropriate ANSI code on the numeric keypad; for example, type **0147** for opening quotes and **0148** for closing quotes. (If you want to create macros that use the Alt+key combinations, you have to locate a chart of the ANSI character codes—these codes aren't listed in the Word or Windows documentation.)

Alternatively, you can choose Insert Symbol. In the Symbols From box, choose the font set that contains the symbol you want. You find typeset quotation marks in the Normal Text font set, near the middle of the fourth row from the top. Double-click the character to insert it and exit the dialog box. Using the Symbol dialog box, you can quickly record macros that insert the special characters.

Use creative design wizardry with type

Contemporary graphic design makes frequent use of typographic gimmicks for an arty, "designed" look. Among these are very wide letter spacing, larger font sizes used in the middle of a word, and individual letters placed above the baseline of a word. You can automate this kind of artfulness with the subscript, superscript, and letter spacing features.

To adjust the amount of subscripting and superscripting, choose Format Character, choose Superscript or Subscript in the Super/subscript box, and then type a measurement in the By box. (To format existing text, select the text first.) Larger numbers place subscript and superscript characters farther beneath and above the baseline, respectively. To format text with extra spacing, choose Format Character Spacing Expanded, and type a measurement in the By box. Then choose OK. (You can specify measurements to a quarter of a point.) Word shows the effect of your changes in the Sample box. To automate the process further, assign your "oddball" character formatting choices to styles.

Use special effects with Dingbats and Wingdings

You can change the size of decorative symbol characters (such as Zapf Dingbats or Wingdings) by selecting the character and using the Format Character command or the point size box in the ribbon. You often can obtain an interesting "designed" effect by applying italic formatting to a Dingbat or Wingding character. To remove character formatting from the character, press Ctrl+space bar.

Note: If the symbol is contained in a protected field, updating all fields in the document may remove the formatting you have applied.

Avoid desktop-publishing drudgery

Word makes light work of a very tedious desktop publishing task: formatting repetitive material such as catalogs, price lists, phone directories, spec sheets, employee directories, and so on. To simplify and speed the formatting of such lists, use the Next Style feature to automatically format body text after a heading. Choose Format Style Define, type or select the heading name, and choose or type a style name in the Next Style box. Then choose Change and choose Yes when Word asks if you want to change the standard style. Choose Close to return to the document. When you apply the heading style and press Enter at the end of a heading, Word automatically switches to the next style.

Use tables to create complex forms

You can use the Tables feature to create extremely complex forms—all it takes is a little bit of planning. The basic procedure is to draw the form on paper, then create a table with a sufficient number of columns to accommodate all the data entry cells. Keep in mind that it's a lot easier to merge cells than to split them, because Word doesn't let you split cells that haven't been merged first. It's better to err on the side of having too many columns than too few; although you will save time by specifying the exact number of columns you need. After creating the basic table, you can merge cells and move and format cell borders to create the form. To shade a cell, select the cell by clicking its left border, choose Format Border Shading and specify the kind of shading you want, and then choose OK twice.

Use truncated type to produce arty effects

To create arty, "designed" effects with type, place the type in a table, then select the table row that contains the type. Choose Table Row Height Exactly, and specify a row height that's smaller than the row's text. Word truncates the tops and bottoms of the letter when you print the page. For other interesting effects, try shading cells and formatting cells with borders.

Balance columns easily

A task you will encounter frequently when laying out desktop published documents is the necessity to balance columns so they align at their bottom edges, or so one column ends with sufficient space left for a boxed advertisement, pull-quote, and so on. To perform this task efficiently, you need to see most of the page. To zoom in on the page, switch to Page Layout view so columns are displayed side by side, then choose View Zoom 50% and OK. To insert a column break, position the insertion point and press Ctrl+Shift+Enter, or choose Insert Break Column Break and OK. To align columns evenly at the bottom, move the insertion point to the end of the text and choose Insert Break, choose Continuous in the Section Break box, and choose OK.

Put columns in boxes

You can put columns of text in boxes, but you must create a box for each column. The process, therefore, is not very suitable for long documents. Follow these steps to place a column in a box:

1. Choose Format Columns, type a number in the Number of Columns box, and choose OK.

2. Choose Format Border Box, choose a line pattern, and choose OK.
3. Type the text of the column.

Repeat steps 1-3 for each new column of text.

Apply shading

You can apply gray shading to frames, table cells, or selected text. Select the cell, frame, or text you want to shade, and choose Format Border Shading. Select a shading pattern and choose OK, then choose Line and Border styles, and choose OK again. To shade only the text in a cell, select only the text, not the cell. (This trick doesn't work with frames; Word applies shading to the entire frame, whether you select text or not.)

Make shaded text legible

If misused, shading can destroy the legibility of your documents. Graphic designers have developed useful rules for shaded text. To ensure legibility, never use shading darker than 5%. (The WinWord User's Guide recommends that you try 20% shading, which would mean that no one would be able to read your message.) Use a large font (at least 12 points), and choose sans serif text or a boldfaced serif font. (Fine serifs tend to disappear when shaded.)

Use on-screen guides for desktop publishing

When desktop publishing in Word, be sure to turn on text boundaries. With boundaries turned on, Word displays the margins of text columns, headers and footers, footnotes, and so on. This capability helps you place page elements precisely. Choose Tools Options, press V to select View options, and select Text Boundaries in the

Show Text with box. While you're in the View Options screen, select the Line Breaks and Fonts as Printed and Table Gridlines check boxes to further enhance the accuracy of text placement.

Edit WordArt objects

The WordArt program supplied with Word 2.0 enables you to create moderately interesting special effects with type, such as placing text vertically on the page, arching and slanting type, and printing type upside down. You can vastly extend the range of special effects by editing WordArt objects with Microsoft Draw, another application that comes with Word.

First, create the object with WordArt. Choose Insert Object, and choose Microsoft WordArt and OK. In the WordArt dialog box, choose a font and any desired special effects, then choose Apply and OK. Word inserts the object into your document. You now can enlarge, shrink, and stretch the WordArt object by clicking it and dragging its frame handles.

To edit the WordArt object in Draw, click the object, then press Ctrl+Shift+F9 to unlink it from WordArt. Next, double-click the object or choose Edit Picture. Word displays the object in the Microsoft Draw editing screen. Notice that each letter is a separate object in Draw, with its own selection handles. To make it easier to work with each separate letter, maximize the Draw window and choose View, 200%, 400%, or 800%. Any changes you make in Draw will be reflected in the object when you choose File Exit and Return to *document name*, then choose Yes in the Update *filename*? dialog box.

Note: You can't edit Equation Editor objects with Draw, which treats equations as text.

Create pull-quotes

Word enables you to quickly create *pull-quotes*—text and itemized lists in framed boxes apart from body text. To create a framed pull-quote follow these steps:

1. Select the text you want to frame.

2. Click the Frame button on the toolbar, or choose Insert Frame. (The Frame button is the ninth button from the right in the toolbar as installed; it looks like a U.S. flag.)

   Word places the text in the frame.

3. To move the frame, click in a frame border (but not on a frame handle) until the cursor turns into a four-pronged arrow, then drag-and-drop the frame to a new location.

4. To resize the frame, click the frame to display frame handles, then drag frame handles to the desired size.

5. To format the frame with custom borders and shading, choose Format Border. Select a line in the Line box, then choose Shading, Custom, select options in the Pattern, Foreground, and Background boxes, then choose OK twice.

Be careful when using shading over text. On laser printers, shading darker than 5% may make the text hard to read; for typeset text, 10% may still be readable. For best readability, experiment with font sizes, serif and sans serif fonts, and boldfacing.

Create reversed (black-on-white) pull-quotes

You can format pull-quotes and other framed text with reversed type (black-on-white). Be careful when you use this technique—reversed text can be hard to read with inappropriate fonts and font sizes. In general, choose a sans serif font like Helvetica, because fine serifs may become "plugged" with ink. Also, small font sizes (for example, 10-point text) may be hard to read. Test readability using boldfaced 12-point Helvetica for starters.

To create reversed type, follow these steps:

1. Create the text and the frame as described in the previous tip.
2. Choose Format **B**order **S**hading **C**ustom. Choose Clear in the **P**attern box, White in the **F**oreground box, and Black in the **B**ackground box. Choose OK twice to return to the document window.

   Don't panic when you see that the text has "disappeared" because you've specified black type on a black background. In the next step, you will specify white characters:
3. Choose Format **C**haracter, choose White in the **C**olor box, and choose OK.

The frame now contains reversed type. To find the most readable type, select the text in the frame and choose various fonts and sizes. When you choose a larger font, the frame automatically expands to accommodate the text. If the box extends past the end of the current page, Word moves the box to the next page. To split the box, create a new frame on the following page and cut and paste some of the text into it.

Use reversed type rarely

Reversed text (white text on a black background) lowers reading comprehension by 30%. For optimal readability, use reversed type with a 100% black background only.

Crop graphics in Word 2.0 and later versions

In Word 1.X, dragging frame handles crops a picture rather than scaling it. To crop a picture in Word 2.0 and later versions, hold down Shift while you drag the handle.

Import graphic formats with Word

To check which graphic import filters have been installed, choose Tools Options, press W to choose WIN.INI, and choose MS Graphic Import Filters in the Application list box. Word displays the installed graphic filters in the Startup Options box.

Position captions

For your desktop published documents, you may want to use photos that have captions positioned above, beneath, or to the side. The easiest way to position captions is with a table. Load a graphic image in a cell, or shade a cell 100% black to create a photo indicator for the printer, then type the caption in a cell above, below, or to the side of the illustration.

Add space above a frame

If you create a frame at the top of a document and want to add text above it, position the insertion point to the left of the frame and press Ctrl+Shift+Enter.

Size Excel charts in Word

If you import a Microsoft Excel chart with the Clipboard and try to resize it in Word, the chart may look unattractive. The solution is to size charts in Excel before importing them.

Import documents that use Line Draw

Word doesn't have a Line Draw feature, and Line Draw characters in documents you import from other word processor formats are converted to vertical and horizontal bars from the ANSI character set. To create line drawings, choose Insert Object, and choose Microsoft Drawing and OK. Create the drawing in Microsoft Draw, then choose File Exit and Return to *filename.* Then choose Yes at the Update Filename dialog box. Word places the drawing in a frame.

15

CHAPTER

Linking Word with Other Applications

One of Microsoft Windows most widely appreciated benefits is the capability to transfer data quickly from one program to another via the Windows Clipboard. Many programs now also support DDE (Dynamic Data Exchange) and OLE (Object Linking and Embedding—pronounced olé). With DDE, for example, you can set up a link that automatically updates a Microsoft Excel spreadsheet embedded in a Word document when you change the source data in Excel. With OLE, you quickly can edit objects created with Microsoft mini-applications such as Microsoft Draw, which are supplied with Word. This chapter covers tips for linking and for importing and exporting files between Word and other applications.

Customize Word to link external file formats

To open external data in Word, such as dBASE files or Excel worksheets, you must first install the corresponding file converter. If you didn't install the correct converter files when you installed Word, rerun the installation program by choosing the Word Setup program icon in the Word for Windows program group of the Windows Program Manager. Then choose the customized installation option and choose to install the appropriate file converters. (You will need your original installation disks so Word can copy the files it needs.)

Turn off links to prevent unwanted updating

When you link information that's updated often but seldom printed—for example, itemized purchases that will be printed in monthly billings—you will not want to update the link in the destination document (a billing statement) every time the data changes. To lock links, follow these steps:

1. Press Ctrl+F11 (Lock Field) with the cursor in a link field, or choose Edit Links, select the links you want to lock, and choose Locked and OK.

   To unlock links at print-time:

2. Choose Edit Links, select the links, clear the Locked check box, and choose OK.

Be careful when working around link fields

Be careful when editing documents that contain linked information. If you edit a linked destination field, and the source data subsequently changes, Word scraps your editing changes when you update the link. It's much safer to edit the source data. To move quickly to the source of a link, move the insertion point anywhere in the destination field and choose Edit Go To, or press F5. Word displays the Go To dialog box with the destination and source links listed. Choose the source link and OK.

Check the source document when links go bad

If a link goes on the fritz (Word displays an error message when you try to update the link), check whether the source document has been renamed, moved to another directory, or deleted. After you determine the current status of the source document, follow these steps to update the link:

1. Choose Edit Links, choose the link you want to update, choose Change Link, and type the current location of the source file in the File Name box.
2. Choose OK and Update Now.

If the source or destination file was created with another application, Word may ask if you want to re-create the link. Choose Yes.

If the link still doesn't work and it was created in Excel, make sure that you didn't accidentally choose the Ignore Remote Requests option in Excel. Switch to Excel and choose Options Workspace, and clear the Ignore Remote Requests check box.

Use internal links to update repetitive text easily

To have Word automatically update text throughout your document (dates, personnel titles, and so on), you can use an internal link or cross-references.

If you want to update references selectively, use links because you can choose only the links you want updated in the Links dialog box.

References have the advantage that you can give them descriptive names and view them in a convenient list, whereas it may be hard to remember which numbered links refer to which data—especially if you haven't edited a linked document for a long time.

Creating references is easy. Follow these steps:

1. Select the source data (a date, for example) and choose Insert Bookmark (Ctrl+Shift+F5).
2. Type a name for the bookmark and choose OK.
3. To insert a cross-reference, position the insertion point at the new location and choose Insert Field. Then press R to select Reference in the Insert Field Type list.
4. In the Instructions box, choose the bookmark name, then choose Add and OK.

Create references "manually"

A quicker but potentially error-prone way to create references (because it's manual) is to perform the following procedure:

1. Turn on the display of field codes (choose View Field Codes).
2. Press Ctrl+F9 to insert field code brackets ({}).
3. Type the reference code (for example: **{REF DATE}**).
4. To update all references in a document, press Ctrl+5 on the numeric keypad to select the whole document, then press F9 (Update Field).

Update text with internal links

If you create documents with repetitive information that changes over time, you can use the link feature to automatically update all references within the same document or within several Word documents. You can, for example, use internal links to change part numbers, dollar amounts, or the names of persons in a contract. To update references by using the link feature, follow these steps:

1. Select the information you want to link and choose Edit Copy (Ctrl+C).

2. Move the insertion point where you want the information reinserted and choose Edit Paste Special Formatted Text Paste Link.

3. To insert other copies of the link, choose View, make sure that the Field Codes item is checked, return to the document screen, select the link field, and choose Edit Copy (Ctrl+C).

4. Move to each insertion point for the linked text and choose Edit Paste (Ctrl+V).

   When you edit the original text, you must update the link manually.

5. Press Ctrl+5 on the numeric keypad to select the whole document, then press F9 to update all links. Alternatively, you can choose Edit Links, select the links to update from the Edit Links dialog box, and choose Update Now. Word changes the text throughout thc document.

Print an embedded spreadsheet in landscape mode on its own page

To include an embedded worksheet that's wider than the 8.5 inch page width, you can tell Word to print it on a separate page in Landscape mode. Follow these steps:

1. Select the worksheet and choose Format Page Setup.

2. Choose Size and Orientation and choose Selected Text in the Apply to box.

3. Choose Landscape and OK.

To view your work, choose File Print Preview Two Pages, and then choose Close.

Import data from Microsoft Excel

To import data from a Microsoft Excel spreadsheet, follow these steps:

1. From Word for Windows, switch to Program Manager and start Excel.
2. In Excel, choose File Open, choose a file, and choose OK.
3. Highlight the cells you want to copy into Word.
4. Choose Options Display Row and Column Headings to deselect headings, and choose OK.
5. Choose Edit Copy.
6. Switch back to Word for Windows.
7. Open a Word document and position the cursor where you want to insert the Excel data.
8. Choose Edit Paste Special, choose Microsoft Excel Worksheet Object, and choose Paste.

To insert the Excel data as a picture, in step 8 choose Edit Paste Special, choose Picture in the Data Type box, and choose Paste Link.

16

CHAPTER

Using Word Macros

Macros are marvelous! When you find yourself repeating the same task in Word over and over, you can save time and frustration by recording those keystrokes and commands in a macro. After you press the macro's invocation key (or select the macro by its name from a list), Word plays back all the recorded keystrokes automatically.

Word for Windows can "record" a macro while you select commands with the mouse or type text at the keyboard. Word also includes an extremely powerful programming language and built-in macro editor you can use to automate the complex tasks. Once you have written a macro, you can assign it to a shortcut key or place it on a Word drop-down menu.

Create a macro button

You can place buttons in your document that, when clicked with the mouse, run a macro you have linked to the button. This capability is a convenient way to organize large directories. Macro buttons in a table of contents, for example, can move the insertion point to the corresponding parts of the document.

Follow these steps to create a macro button:

1. Choose Insert Field, and choose Macro Button in the Insert Field Type list.

2. In the Field Code window, type the name of the macro that you want the button to run. You also can type, in quotes, any text that you want the button to display, and then choose OK (see fig. 16.1).

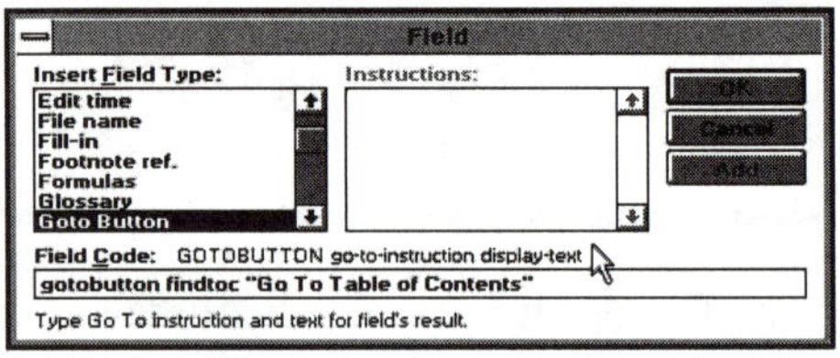

Fig. 16.1 *Field Code window.*

Create pop-up dialog boxes

You easily can create a Word dialog box that displays the time of day. The process makes an excellent tutorial for creating pop-up dialog boxes.

Follow these steps to create the Time dialog box:

1. Choose Tools Macro, type a name (for example, **Time**), and choose Edit.

   Word displays the macro editor.

2. Between the Sub MAIN and End Sub lines (which are required for all macros), type the macro as shown here:

```
Sub MAIN
A$ = Time$( )
B$ = "The time is " + A$
MsgBox B$, "Time",0
End Sub
```

The macro creates a dialog box titled `Time` that displays the message `The time is` and displays the current time. (Remember that if your computer's system time is incorrect, the displayed time also is incorrect.)

3. After you finish typing the macro, choose **F**ile **C**lose, and choose **Y**es at the prompt to save your changes globally. (This action makes the Time dialog box available for all documents.)

You can assign the dialog box to a menu item or a shortcut key. To place the dialog box in a menu, follow these steps:

1. Choose T**o**ols **O**ptions, and press M to display the Menus options.

2. Choose **G**lobal to make the dialog box available for all documents.

3. Choose the **M**acros button, and choose Time in the Macro**s** list box.

4. Choose a menu in the Men**u** list box, then choose **A**dd and Close.

When you choose Time from the menu you have selected, a dialog box displays the time. To close the dialog box, choose OK or press Esc.

To assign the dialog box to a shortcut key, follow these steps:

1. Choose T**o**ols **O**ptions, and press K to display the Keyboard options.

2. Choose the **G**lobal button to make the dialog box available for all documents.

3. Choose the Macros button and choose the Time macro in the macros list box.

4. Choose a shortcut key in the Shortcut Key box, and then choose Add and Close.

Create a document cascade macro

If you frequently work with several documents at a time, you may find it convenient to have the documents "cascaded" on the screen. Cascaded document windows are displayed in layers, with each document's title bar visible, enabling the user to switch to any document by clicking its title with the mouse.

When you choose Window Arrange All with several open documents, Word "tiles" the windows (displays each document in its own window), with the result that each window may be too small for efficient editing.

The following macro cascades any open document windows. You can assign the macro to a Toolbar button, as described later.

To create the macro, follow these steps:

1. Choose Tools Macro, type a name for the macro (for example, **Cascade**), and choose Edit.
2. In the macro editor, type the macro as follows. Be very careful not to insert any extra spaces.

```
Sub MAIN
Zoom = SelInfo(19)
Outline = ViewOutline( )
ViewZoom100
If DocMaximize( ) Then DocMaximize
NumWindows = CountWindows( ) - 1
VLap = 14
HLap = 7
Width = Val(AppInfo$(6)) - NumWindows * HLap
Height = Val(AppInfo$(7)) - NumWindows * VLap
```

```
For Cascade = 1 To NumWindows + 1
NextWindow
DocMove NewWidth, NewHeight
DocSize Width, Height
NewWidth = NewWidth + HLap
NewHeight = NewHeight + VLap
Next Cascade
ViewZoom .ZoomPercent = Zoom
If Outline Then ViewOutline
bye:
End Sub
```

3. Choose **F**ile **C**lose, and choose **Y**es to save changes globally.
4. To run the macro, choose T**o**ols **M**acro, select the macro's name, and choose **R**un.

   Word cascades all open documents.

To open a cascaded document, click its title bar. To rearrange the cascaded documents, click and drag in a document's title bar, or run the Cascade macro again. Word places the currently opened document window at the front of the cascaded pile.

Note: If the macro doesn't run properly, or if Word displays an error message, check your typing carefully. The macro must be entered exactly as shown in step 2.

To assign the macro to a Toolbar button, follow these steps:

1. Choose T**o**ols **O**ptions, and press T to display Toolbar options.
2. In the Show box, make sure that the **M**acros button is selected.
3. In the Macro**s** list box, select the Cascade macro.

4. In the Tool to Change list box, choose a button to reassign to the macro. If you don't want to reassign an existing button, choose `[space]`.
5. In the Button list box, choose a new button for the macro; for example, the C button (for "Cascade").
6. Choose Change Close.

   After you choose the C button in the Toolbar, Word cascades the open documents.

Create a paragraph double-indent macro

One of the most useful macros for Word is one that indents quoted text 0.5 inches (or any distance you specify) from the left and right margins. To create this macro, follow these steps:

1. Choose Tools Record Macro, and type **DoubleIndent** in the Record Macro Name box.
2. Assign an optional shortcut key in the Shortcut Key box, and type a description in the Description box—for example **Left/Right Indent**—and then choose OK

   Word returns you to the document screen and displays REC in the status bar.
3. Choose Format Paragraph, specify .5 in the From Left and From Right boxes, and choose OK.
4. Choose Tools Stop Recorder.

To run the macro, press the shortcut key or choose Tools Macro, choose the macro's name (DoubleIndent, in this example), and choose Run. At the end of the indented text, press Ctrl+S or click Normal style in the ribbon, and press Enter. Choose No in response to the prompt to redefine Normal style.

Use automatic macros

Automatic macros are a special class of macros that run when you issue a given command. All you have to do to create an automatic macro is record or write a macro and then give it one of the names from the following table.

Name	Action
AutoExec	Runs when you start Word
AutoNew	Runs when you create a new document
AutoOpen	Runs when you open a document
AutoClose	Runs when you close a document
AutoExit	Runs when you exit Word

The specific steps to create an automatic macro are as follows:

1. Choose T**o**ols **R**ecord Macro. Type one of the automatic macro names and choose a shortcut key, if desired. Then choose OK. The status bar displays REC.
2. Type the keys and commands that you want to execute with the macro.
3. Choose T**o**ols Stop **R**ecorder.

You also can create the macro in the macro editor:

1. Choose T**o**ols **M**acro. Type one of the automatic macro names.
2. Choose **E**dit. Program the macro in the macro editor and choose **F**ile **C**lose.

The following tips describe some useful automatic macros.

Use AutoExec to change to a specific directory

By default, Word starts in the C:\WINWORD directory and saves documents in the same directory. An AutoExec macro can make Word save your documents in another directory.

The first step is to record a macro. The macro will not do exactly what you want, but you will use it as a basis for later fine-tuning with the Word macro editor.

1. Open a new document and choose Tools Record Macro.
2. Name the macro AutoExec, type a description and choose a shortcut key, if desired, and then choose OK.
3. Choose File Open and change to the directory you want Word to use for saving documents.
4. Open any file, then choose Tools Stop Recorder.
5. Choose Tools Macro, choose AutoExec in the Macro Name list, and choose Edit.
6. In the macro editor, remove the line beginning with `FileOpen`, which indicates the name of the file you opened in step 4.

   The macro editing window should now show the following:

   ```
   Sub MAIN
   ChDir "C\directory you specified in step 3"
   End Sub
   ```

Use AutoOpen to return to a prior location in a document

The following macro automatically returns you to the insertion point where you were working before you closed a document.

1. Choose Tools Record Macro.
2. Type **AutoOpen** in the Record Macro Name box.
3. Choose a shortcut key and type a description, if desired, and choose OK.
4. Press Shift+F5.
5. Choose Tools Stop Recorder.

If you open the macro in the macro recorder, you see that it consists of just the following three lines:

```
Sub MAIN
GoBack
End Sub
```

To save the macro, choose File Close Yes. When you exit Word, choose Yes when prompted to save global glossary and command changes.

Create a template macro that inserts the date and time

This macro may be useful if you keep a journal. When you open a file that uses the journal template, the macro moves the cursor to the end of the file and inserts the date and time. (Remember to set your computer's system date and time correctly, or Word will display the incorrect time and date.)

Before you record the macro, create a template to use for journal entries. Follow these steps:

1. Choose File New, choose the Template button in the New box, and choose OK.

2. Create the template.

   You can include any of these features in a template: text and graphics, page layout and character formatting, styles, keyboard and menu modifications, glossary entries, and macros.

3. Choose File Template, and in the Store New Macros and Glossaries as box, choose With Document Template. Then choose OK.

4. Choose File Save, type a name for the template in the File Name box, and choose OK. Choose OK again if Word displays the Summary Info dialog box.

Word saves the template with a DOT extension in the Word program directory unless you specify another location.

Any template-specific macros you create are available only when you attach a document to the new template. The macros are not listed in the Macro dialog box with other templates loaded.

Record the macro that inserts the date and time. Follow these steps:

1. Choose Tools Record Macro.

2. Name the macro AutoOpen.

3. Type a description and shortcut key, if desired, then choose OK.

4. Press Ctrl+End to move the insertion point to the end of the document.

5. Press Enter twice to insert a blank line and begin a new paragraph.

6. Press Alt+Shift+D to insert today's date.

7. Press Shift+F11 (or Alt+Shift+F1) to select the date field.

8. Press Ctrl+Shift+F9 to replace the field with its result (the text of today's date).
9. Press End to move to the end of the line.
10. Press comma, space bar, and press Alt+Shift+T to insert the time.
11. Press Shift+F11 (or Alt+Shift+F1) to select the time field.
12. Press Ctrl+Shift+F9 to replace the field with its result (the text of the current time).
13. Choose heading1 from the style pull-down menu on the ribbon.
14. Press End to move to the end of the line.
15. Press Enter to begin a new paragraph.
16. Choose Tools Stop Recorder.
17. When you exit Word, choose Yes at the prompt to save glossary and command changes.

Use AutoNew to insert the author's name in a footer

You can have Word insert your name in a footer when you create a new document.

First, create a new template by following these steps:

1. Choose File New, choose the Template button in the New box, and choose OK.
2. Create the template.

   You can include any of these features in a template: text and graphics, page layout and character formatting, styles, keyboard and menu modifications, glossary entries, and macros.

3. Choose File Template, and in the Store New Macros and Glossaries as box, choose With Document Template. Then choose OK.
4. Choose File Save, type a name for the template in the File Name box, and choose OK. Choose OK again if Word displays the Summary Info dialog box.

Word saves the template with a DOT extension in the Word program directory unless you specify another location.

Any template-specific macros you create are available only when you attach a document to the new template. The macros are not listed in the Macro dialog box with other templates loaded.

Follow these steps before recording the macro:

1. Choose Tools Options, press U to get User Info from the Category box, and make sure that your name is typed correctly in the Name box. Then choose OK.
2. Choose Format Style, and define a Footer style if you want to use a particular font and spacing for the footer.
3. Choose View Normal.

Now record the macro by following these steps:

1. Choose Tools Record Macro.
2. Name the macro AutoNew.
3. Type a description, if desired, and choose OK.
4. Choose View Header/Footer.
5. Choose Different First Page.
6. Choose Footer and OK.
7. In the Footer pane, choose Insert Field.

8. Choose the Author field in the Insert Field Type list and choose OK.

9. Choose Close to exit the Footer pane.

10. Choose Tools Stop Recorder.

11. Choose File Save, type a name for the new template, and choose OK. Choose OK again if Word displays the Summary Info dialog box.

12. When you exit Word, choose Yes at the prompt to save glossary and command changes.

Use AutoClose to open the summary information dialog box when you close a document

To create a macro that automatically opens the summary information dialog box when you close a document, follow these steps:

1. Choose Tools Macro.

2. Name the macro AutoClose and type a description, then choose Edit.

3. Type:

   On Error Resume Next

4. Press Enter and type the following line between the `Sub MAIN` and `End Sub` lines:

   ToolsMacro .name="FileSummaryInfo",.Run

5. Choose File Close, and choose Yes at the prompt to keep changes.

When you close a document, Word displays the Summary Info dialog box for the document.

Create macros that work globally or with a specific template

You can create macros that are available for all documents or for only one template. With the default NORMAL.DOT template loaded, you can create only global macros.

To create a template-specific macro, follow these steps:

1. Choose **F**ile **N**ew, choose the **T**emplate button in the New box, and choose OK.
2. Create the template.

   You can include any of these features in a template: text and graphics, page layout and character formatting, styles, keyboard and menu modifications, glossary entries, and macros.
3. Choose **F**ile **T**emplate and in the Store New Macros and Glossaries as box, choose With Document **T**emplate. Then choose OK.
4. Choose **F**ile **S**ave, type a name for the template in the File **N**ame box, and choose OK. Choose OK again if Word displays the Summary Info dialog box.

Word saves the template with a DOT extension in the Word program directory unless you specify another location.

Any template-specific macros you create are available only when you attach a document to the new template. The macros will not be listed in the Macro dialog box with other templates loaded.

Prevent automatic macros from running

To prevent an automatic macro from running, hold down Shift while you perform the action that runs the macro. To prevent AutoOpen from running when you open a document, for example, hold down Shift while you choose OK after choosing **File Open**.

17

CHAPTER

Customizing Word for Windows

Word for Windows is among the most easily customized word processors available today. You can use macros to customize Word, as described in the preceding chapter, and then assign the macros to menu items and dialog boxes of your own. You can add and remove buttons from the Toolbar. You also can use the customization features of Windows to make Word work exactly as you want, as this chapter describes.

Use templates to customize Word without confusing other users

To customize Word's menus, keyboard assignments, and Toolbar buttons without confusing others who use the same copy of Word, assign customized features to templates rather than globally.

Customize your Word menus

Adding customized commands to Word's existing menus is surprisingly easy. You can, for example, add menu items that run macros.

Before adding anything to a menu, save a backup copy of the file NORMAL.DOT, located in the WINWORD subdirectory. You can name the backup copy NORMAL.BAK, for example.

To assign a macro to a menu item, follow these steps:

1. Record the macro, and then choose the Tools Stop Recorder.
2. Choose Tools Options, and press M to display the Menu options.
3. In the Show box, choose the Macros button.
4. In the Context box, choose Global.
5. In the Menu list, highlight the name of the menu to which you want to assign the macro.
6. In the Macros list, highlight the name of the macro you want to assign to a menu, and then choose Add.

   Note: If you want the new menu item separated by a dashed line from the other menu items above it, first highlight the dashed line in the Macros list, and choose Add. Then choose the name of the macro and choose Add again.
7. In the Menu Text box, type the text of the new menu item.

   Word makes the first letter of the menu item its hot key by default. To assign a different letter as the menu item's hot key, insert an ampersand (&) in front of the letter for the hot key. For example, if you type **Era&sefile** as the menu item's name, Word makes the letter *s* the new menu item's hot key and underlines it on the menu.
8. Choose Close.

9. When you exit Word, choose Yes when prompted to save global, glossary, and command changes, or any changes in the attached template.

Create a quick insert key

If you rarely or never use Word's Overtype mode, you can redefine the normal toggle function of the Ins key from Overtype to Paste so that you can use it to paste text from the Clipboard. Choose the Tools Options command, press G to display the General options, and then select the Use the INS Key for Paste check box. Then choose OK.

Use items deleted from customized menus

Suppose you have removed what you thought were unneeded menu items from the custom templates you created to use on specialized documents. But now you need to use one of the deleted menu commands. Choose the Tools Macro command, and click the Commands button. Then select the desired command from the list and choose Run.

Edit system files without leaving Word for Windows

Word enables you to edit the important WIN.INI system configuration file without leaving the program. Choose the Tools Options command, and select WIN.INI in the Category list box. In the Startup Options list box, move the cursor to the line you want to edit, and then make your changes in the Setting text box. Choose Close. To edit WIN.INI settings for other programs, select the appropriate application in the Application drop-down text box.

You can edit system files in Word's editing window, too, as long as you remember to save them in DOS text (ASCII) format.

Install the Windows System Editor to edit system files

You also can edit your SYSTEM.INI, CONFIG.SYS, and AUTOEXEC.BAT files by installing the Windows System Configuration Editor. To add the editor to the Applications group, follow these steps:

1. Press Alt+Esc to switch to the Windows Program Manager.
2. Choose File New.
3. In the New Program Object dialog box, choose the Program Item button, and then choose OK.
4. In the Description box, type **system editor**; in the Command Line box, type **sysedit**. (Add path specifications as needed.) Choose OK.

Windows adds the System Editor icon to the Applications group.

Follow these steps to use the System Configuration Editor to edit your system files:

1. If you're not already there, switch to the Applications group in the Windows Program Manager.
2. Double-click the System Editor icon.

   Windows loads all four system files (AUTOEXEC.BAT, CONFIG.SYS, WIN.INI, and SYSTEM.INI) in stacked windows.

3. To edit a file, click in its window.
4. To locate a particular section of a long system file to edit, choose Search Find, type the text you want to find, and then choose Find Next.

   To find the next occurrence of the text in the file, choose Search Next or press F3. To find the previous occurrence, choose Search Previous or press F4.

5. After you finish, choose **File Save** to save the edited file. Then choose **File Exit** to return to Word.

Using the Windows System Configuration Editor to edit system files automatically saves the files in ASCII format.

Note: You must reboot your computer to activate your changes to the AUTOEXEC.BAT and CONFIG.SYS files, and you must reload Windows to activate any changes to WIN.INI and SYSTEM.INI.

Run Word without opening a new document

You can configure Word so that a new document isn't opened every time you run the program. Click the Word for Windows icon in the Windows Program Manager, and then choose **File Properties**. Type a space and **/N** after winword.exe in the **C**ommand Line text box, and then choose OK. (Don't forget the space before **/N**, or you will get an error message.)

Configure Windows to start Word automatically

You can configure Windows 3.1 to start Word automatically when you load Windows.

On installation, Windows creates a program group called Startup. Drag the Word icon into the Startup group, and Windows automatically loads Word and any other programs in the Startup group when you start Windows. If you decided not to use the Startup group and have deleted it, you can create it again. Starting in the Program Manager, choose **File New**, and then choose Program **G**roup and OK. Type **Startup** in the **D**escription box, and choose OK.

To stop Windows from running the programs in the Startup group, hold down the Shift key as Windows loads.

Start Word automatically with the LOAD or RUN commands

You also can add a RUN or LOAD command to the WIN.INI file to load Word automatically when you run Windows. The LOAD command runs the application and minimizes it to an icon. The RUN command opens the program and can even load a specific file if you add the file's name to the end of the RUN command line.

Follow these steps to add RUN or LOAD to the WIN.INI file:

1. Open the WIN.INI file in Word. WIN.INI is located in the C:\WINDOWS directory in the default Windows installation.

   (You can edit WIN.INI in Word, as long as you remember to save it as a DOS text file by using the File Save As command.)

2. Find the `[windows]` section of WIN.INI and enter the LOAD or RUN command on its own line, along with Word's directory path and file name (see the following example).

   The following example loads Word and Microsoft Excel automatically when you run Windows:

   `[windows]`
   run=c:\winword\winword.exe *[you can add a filename here to open a specific file when Word runs]*
   load=c:\excel\excel.exe

3. Save WIN.INI by choosing **File Save As**. In the Save File as Type list, choose DOS Text (*.tx8), and then choose OK.
4. Restart Windows to activate your changes.

Windows runs programs associated with RUN or LOAD statements in the WIN.INI file before loading any programs contained in the Startup program group.

Start Word automatically by autoloading its program group

You can place the Word icon in any program group you choose and set Windows to load all the programs in that group automatically.

Follow these steps to automatically load Word with its entire program group:

1. Load the PROGMAN.INI file (located in the WINDOWS directory) in Windows Notepad, as described in the previous tip for WIN.INI.
2. Find the [Settings] section of PROGMAN.INI and type the following new statement on its own line beneath the [Settings] section title:

   Startup="*group name*"

   Here *group name* is the name of the group you want to start when you run Windows. To load a group named Word Processing Programs, for example, type the following:

   Startup="Word Processing Programs"

   Make sure that you enclose the statement in quotation marks.

3. Save the file and restart Windows to activate your changes.

Adjust your keyboard settings to avoid inserting multiple characters

If you install Word and find that each keystroke inserts multiple characters, you probably need to choose a slower keyboard speed. Press Alt+Esc to switch to the Program Manager. Open the Main program group and run the Control Panel. Choose Keyboard and adjust the settings for Delay Before First Repeat and Repeat Rate.

Turn off the Summary dialog box

If you rarely need to fill in summary information for a file, you can tell Word not to prompt you for summary information. Choose Tools Options, press S to display the Save options, and then deselect the Prompt for Summary Info check box.

So far, so good; but what do you do when you need to save summary information for a specific file? When you're ready to save the file, choose File Save As, and then choose Options. Select the Prompt for Summary Info check box, and then choose OK twice. Word displays the Summary Info dialog box for that file.

Use Normal Save to conserve disk space

If disk space is scarce (as when you need to transfer large documents on floppy disks, for example), you can save files in a format that takes up less space by switching from Fast Save to Normal Save.

To save just one document, you don't need to change the default. Instead, simply choose File Save As and then choose Options. Deselect the Allow Fast Saves check box, and choose OK twice.

Create a left-handed mouse

If you're left-handed, you can reverse the actions of the right and left mouse buttons. Open the Main group and the Control Panel in the Windows Program Manager. Choose the mouse icon. In the Mouse dialog box, choose Swap Left/Right Buttons and then choose OK.

Create a line-spacing Toolbar button

Experienced Word for Windows users may miss the line-spacing Toolbar button of version 1.x. Follow these steps to create a line-spacing button for the Toolbar:

1. Choose Tools Options, and then select Toolbar in the Category list box.
2. In the Tool to Change list box, select [space] or a button to replace.
3. In the Button list box, select a new Toolbar button to assign to the line spacing command. Select an S button, for example, for *Spacing*.
4. In the Show box, choose the Commands button.
5. From the Commands list, select one of the following spacing commands:

SpacePara1	Changes line spacing to single
SpacePara15	Changes line spacing to 1.5
SpacePara2	Changes line spacing to double

6. Choose Change, and then choose Close.
7. When you exit Word, choose Yes at the prompt to save global changes.

Create a Toolbar button to toggle field codes on and off

You can create a macro that turns the field code display on and off and then assign that macro to a Toolbar button. This macro can be useful if you frequently edit field codes and need to switch between displays of fields and results.

To create the macro, follow these steps:

1. Choose Tools Macro, and then type a name for the macro in the Macro Name box (for example, **FieldCodesToggle**).
2. Choose Edit, and in the macro editor, type the macro as follows:

   ```
   Sub MAIN
   Result = ViewFieldCodes()
   If Result = 0 Then
   ViewFieldCodes 1
   Print "Field Codes Toggled ON"
   Else
   ViewFieldCodes 0
   Print "Field Codes Toggled OFF"
   EndIf
   End Sub
   ```

   Caution: Be careful not to insert spaces in the `ViewFieldCodes` WordBasic command or between `ViewFieldCodes` and its following parentheses in the `Result =` line.
3. Choose File Close, and then choose Yes.

To assign the macro to a Toolbar button, follow these steps:

1. Choose Tools Options and press T to display the Toolbar options.

2. Make sure that the **M**acros button in the Show box is selected.

3. In the Macro**s** box, select the FieldCodesToggle macro.

4. In the **T**ool to Change box, choose a button to reassign to the macro. If you don't want to reassign an existing button, choose [space].

5. In the **B**utton list box, choose a new button for the macro—for example, the T button (for *Toggle*).

6. Choose Cha**n**ge, and then choose Close.

Now, when you choose the T button in the Toolbar, Word toggles the display of field codes on or off and displays `Field Codes Toggled OFF` (or `ON`) in the status bar.

Create a Format Paragraph Toolbar button

If you frequently change paragraph specs manually—for example, left and right indentation—creating a Format Paragraph Toolbar button can speed up that task. The following steps demonstrate how to replace the UnIndent button with a Format Paragraph button. (This tip also serves as a tutorial for making other changes to the Toolbar.)

1. Choose T**o**ols **O**ptions (or double-click an empty space in the Toolbar), and then press T to display the Toolbar options.

2. Choose UnIndent in the **T**ool to Change box.

3. Choose the Binoculars button in the **B**utton box (see fig. 17.1).

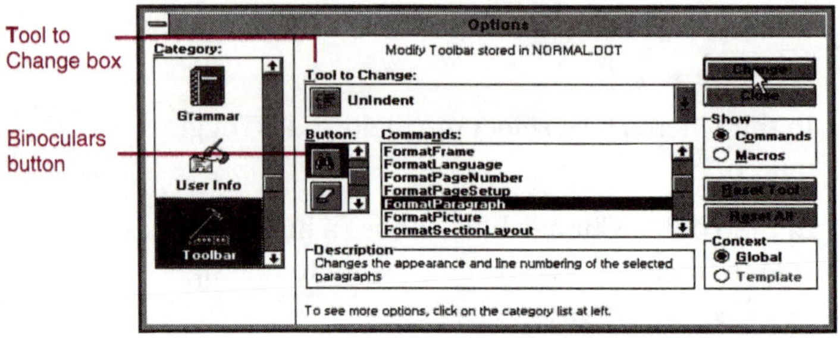

Fig. 17.1 *Toolbar Options dialog box.*

4. Choose the Commands button in the Show box, and select `FormatParagraph` in the Commands box.

5. Choose Change to activate the change and then choose Close to return to the document window.

Now, when you click the Binoculars button in the Toolbar, the Paragraph dialog box appears.

Index

C

D

E

F

G

H

I

K

L

M

N

O

P

Q-R

S

T

U-V

W

X-Z